Music Theory for Singers

Level Seven

Sarah Sandvig

Cover image © Shutterstock, Inc. Used under license.
Back Cover image provided by the author.

Kendall Hunt
publishing company

www.kendallhunt.com
Send all inquiries to:
4050 Westmark Drive
Dubuque, IA 52004-1840

Copyright © 2012 by Sarah Sandvig

ISBN 978-1-4652-0569-8

Kendall Hunt Publishing Company has the exclusive rights to reproduce this work,
to prepare derivative works from this work, to publicly distribute this work,
to publicly perform this work and to publicly display this work.

All rights reserved. No part of this publication may be reproduced,
stored in a retrieval system, or transmitted, in any form or by any
means, electronic, mechanical, photocopying, recording, or otherwise,
without the prior written permission of the copyright owner.

Printed in the United States of America
10 9 8 7 6 5 4 3 2 1

FORWARD

In Sarah Sandvig's *Music Theory for Singers*, voice students and their teachers finally have a singer-friendly primer for musicianship and music theory that is directly applicable to voice training. Mrs. Sandvig has capitalized on her experience as a successful private voice teacher to create this comprehensive workbook, which, in clear, concise language, lays out an easy-to-follow lesson plan progressing from basic through advanced skills. *Music Theory for Singers* is equally applicable in a college or high school classroom setting as in the private studio, and voice teachers will especially appreciate the inclusion of international musical terminology, and music history which their students are likely to encounter in vocal repertoire. For teens studying voice for the first time, as well as for life-long adult singers, *Music Theory for Singers* will become a valued adjunct to any level of vocal study.

Juliana Gondek
Metropolitan Opera soloist and
Prize-winning international recording artist
Professor and Chair, Division of Voice Studies
UCLA

Thank you to the following people for their help and guidance in writing these books: Mary Beard, Melissa Caldretti, Sally Curry, Sharlae Jenkins, Vanessa Parvin, David & Jeanne Sandvig, Connie Venti & my mom and dad, Ken & Christina Watson.

Thank you to my husband Darren and sons Aiden & Caleb for their love, support and patience throughout this writing process.

NOTE TO TEACHER:
These books are a supplement to private, group or class voice lessons, and though I feel these books can stand alone, they are not meant as a replacement for a good teacher for ensuring student learning and understanding of music theory, history, and sight-singing. Each book includes reviews of subjects including a review test (with answers) at the end. Composers, terms and solfege are a unique part of these books that makes them especially helpful for singers. I hope these books can be useful addition to the many teaching tools that already serve to teach young singers in your studio or classroom.

MUSIC THEORY FOR SINGERS
LEVEL 7

BY SARAH SANDVIG

CONTENTS

Review of Concepts in Level 6	1
The Chromatic Scale	3
Enharmonic Notes	4
Review: Chromatic Scale & Enharmonic Notes	5
The Natural minor Scale	9
Minor Key Signatures: g# min., c min., f min.	10
Minor Triads	11
Review: Natural minor Scales & Triads	12
The Appoggiatura, Mordent & Grace Note	15
Rhythm	16
Review: Appoggiatura, Mordent, Grace Note & Rhythm	17
Major Chord Progressions	20
Dominant & Dominant 7 Chords	21
Major & minor Chord Progressions	22
Cadences: Authentic, Plagal & Half	23
Review: Chord Progressions & Cadences	25
Female Voice Classifications	29
Male Voice Classifications	30
Rhythmic Sight-Singing	31
Solfege: Natural minor	32
Review: Voice Classifications & Sight-singing	33
Musical Terms	37
Spotlight on Composers: Enrique Granados	38
Spotlight on Composers: Gabriel Fauré	39
Spotlight on Composers: Aaron Copland	40
Review: Terms & Composers	41
Crossword Puzzle: Musical Terms	42
Level 7 Review Test	44
Review Test: Answers	51
Terms Levels 1-7	55
Diction for Singers	59
References	64

MUSIC THEORY FOR SINGERS
LEVEL 7
REVIEW OF CONCEPTS IN LEVEL 6

Time Signatures

Circle of Fifths

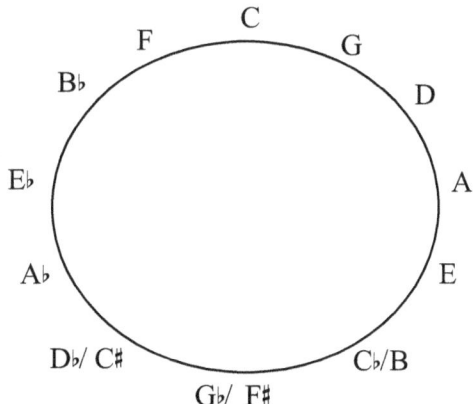

Key Signatures & Triads

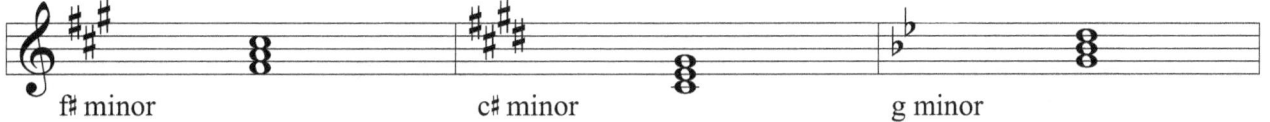

Primary & Secondary Triads

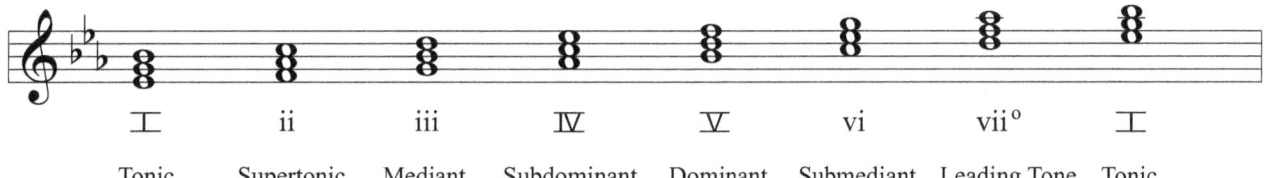

Intervals: Major, minor, diminished & Augmented

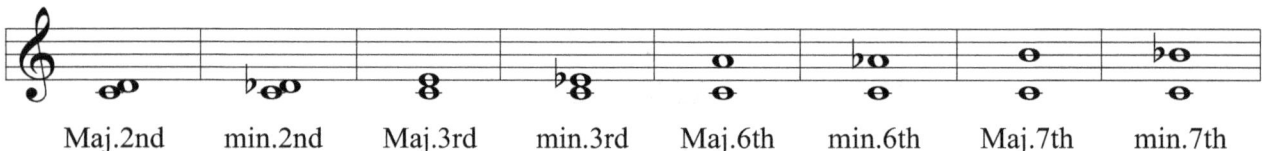

Triads: Major, minor, diminished & Augmented

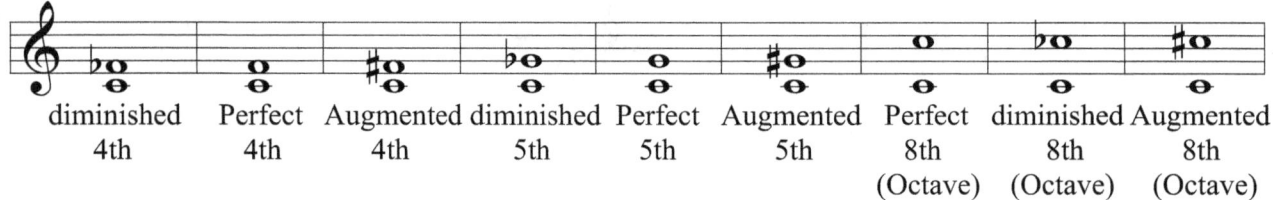

Triads and Inversions

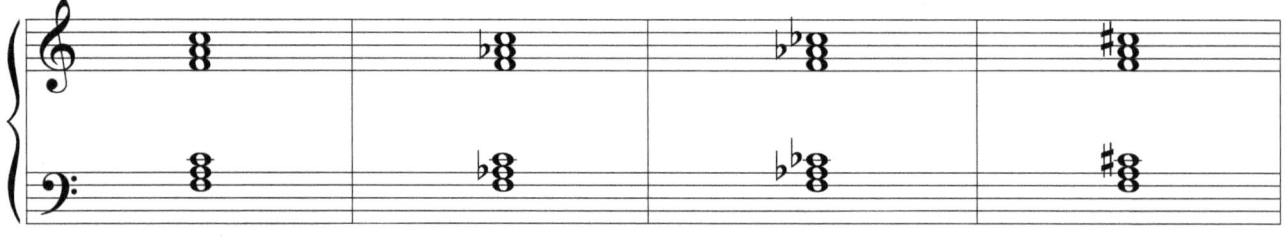

Sight-singing Review

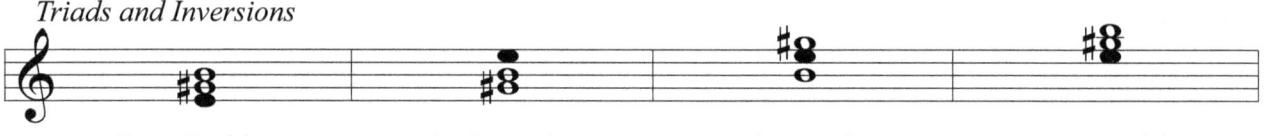

THE CHROMATIC SCALE

A <u>Chromatic Scale</u> is comprised entirely of half steps.
Therefore, an ascending Chromatic scale is: C, C♯, D, D♯, E, F, F♯, G, G♯, A, A♯, B, C.
A descending Chromatic scale is: C, B, B♭, A, A♭, G, G♭, F, E, E♭, D, D♭, C.

Chromatic Scale on the Grand Staff

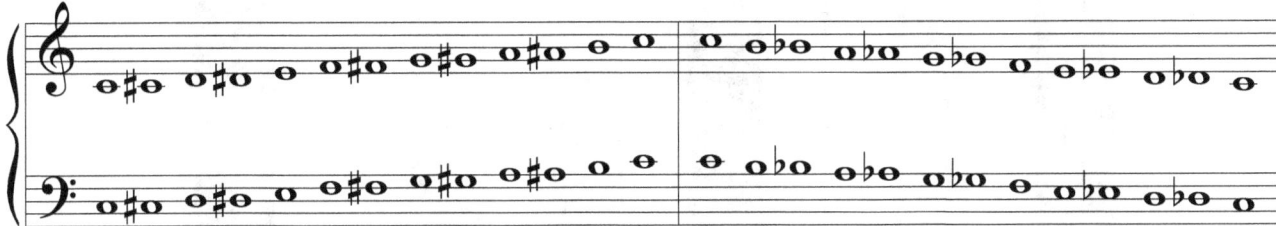

Look at the notes on a piano as well to see the half steps.

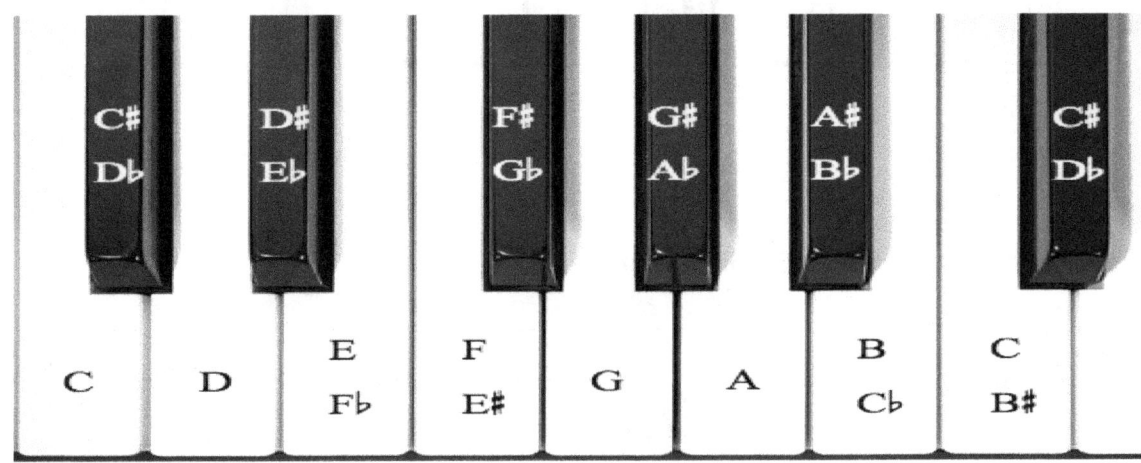

Below is the solfege for a chromatic scale.

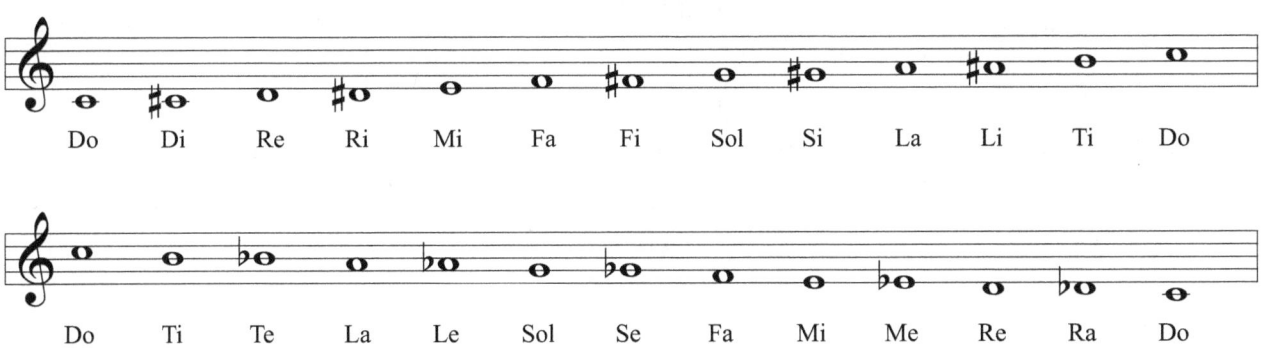

MUSIC THEORY FOR SINGERS

ENHARMONIC NOTES

An <u>Enharmonic Note</u> is the name for two notes that have the same pitch, but different names. For example: F♯ & G♭ have the same pitch (sound the same), but have a different name, depending on what key the music is in. Look at the keyboard below to see all of the enharmonic notes (notes with two names on them).

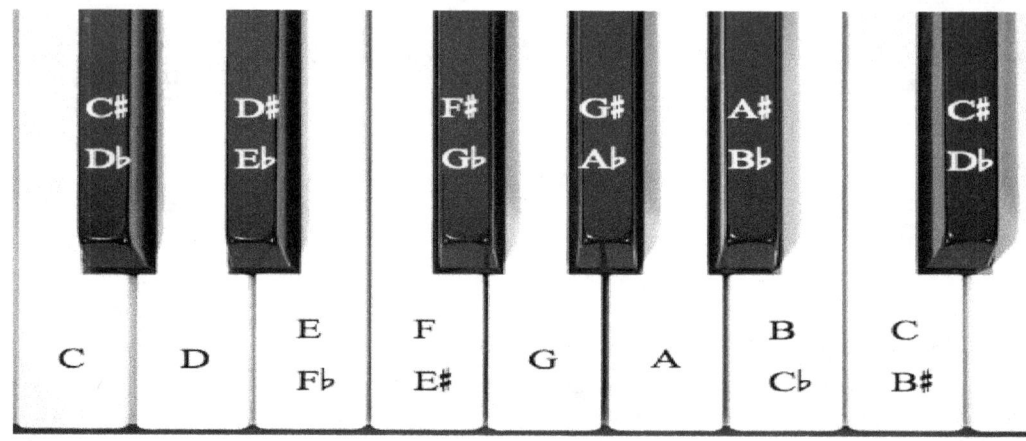

Here are the Enharmonic notes on the Grand Staff.

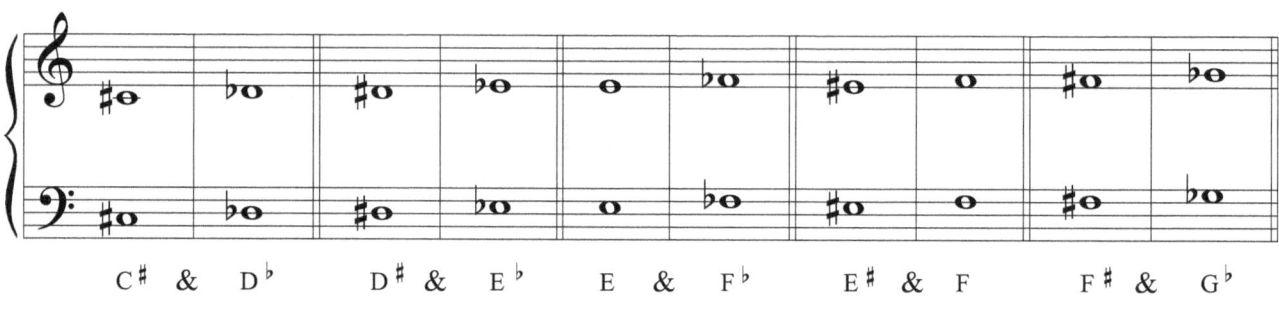

C♯ & D♭   D♯ & E♭   E & F♭   E♯ & F   F♯ & G♭

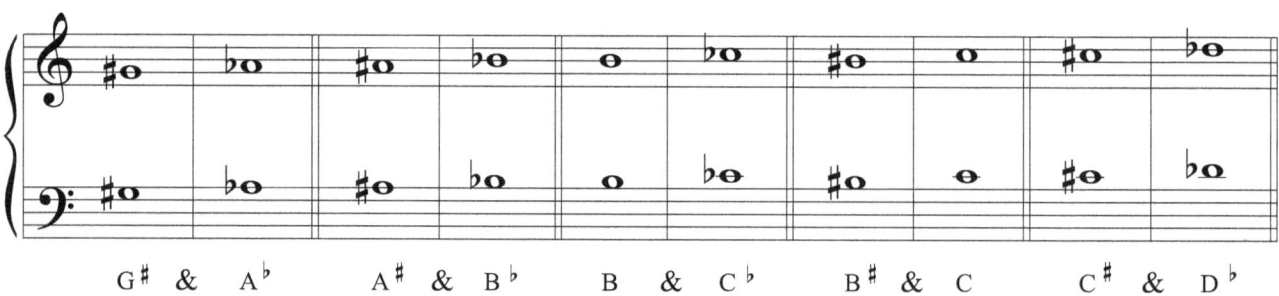

G♯ & A♭   A♯ & B♭   B & C♭   B♯ & C   C♯ & D♭

MUSIC THEORY FOR SINGERS

REVIEW: CHROMATIC SCALE & ENHARMONIC NOTES

1. *Draw <u>ascending</u> chromatic scales on each of the staves below. Notice that each "system" (Grand Staff) starts on a different note. Be careful of the natural half steps (between E-F and B-C). Use whole notes & refer to the keyboard below if you need help.*

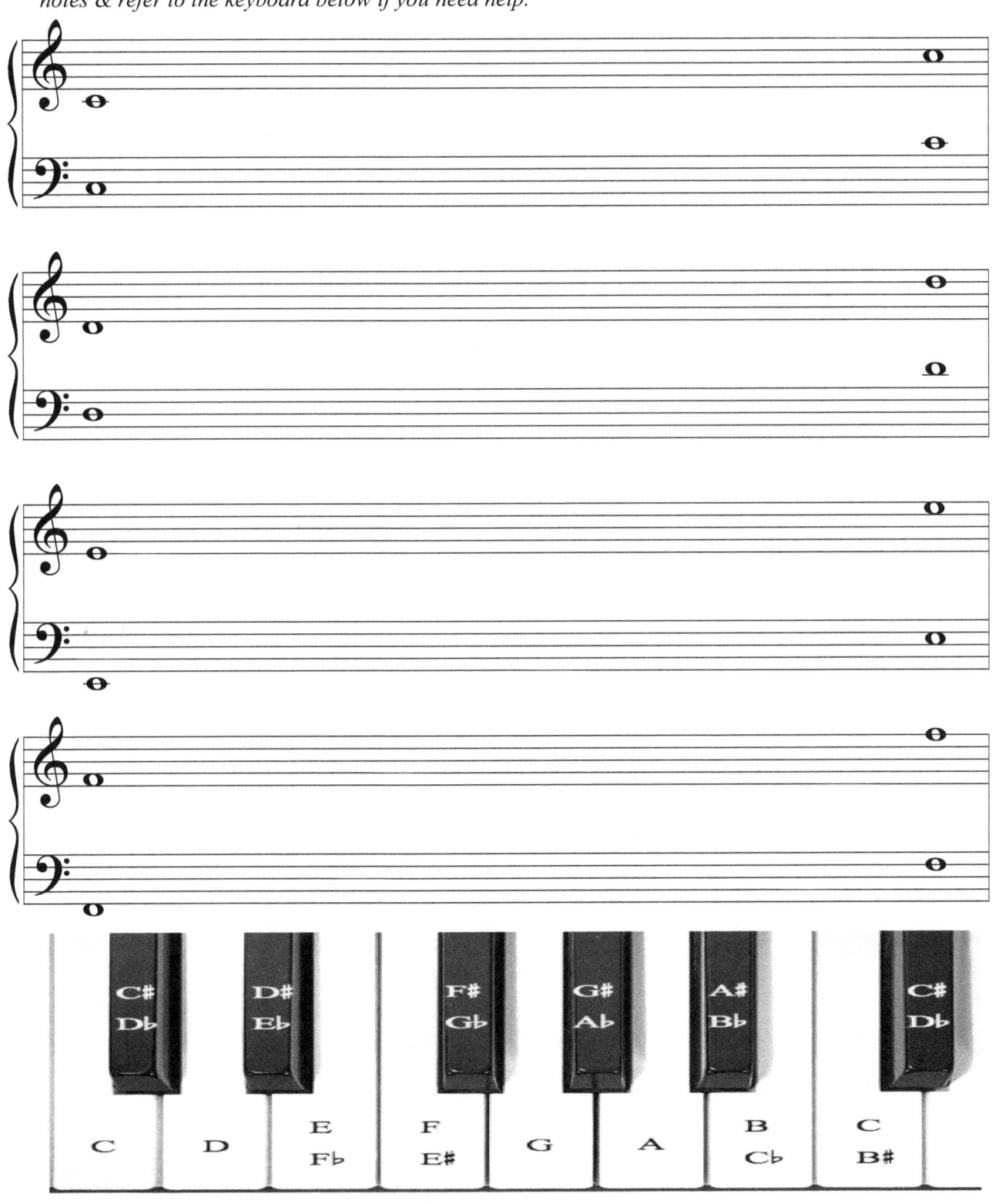

MUSIC THEORY FOR SINGERS

2. Draw *descending* chromatic scales on each of the staves below. Notice that each "system" (Grand Staff) starts on a different note. Be careful of the natural half steps (between E-F and B-C). Use whole notes & refer to the keyboard below if you need help.

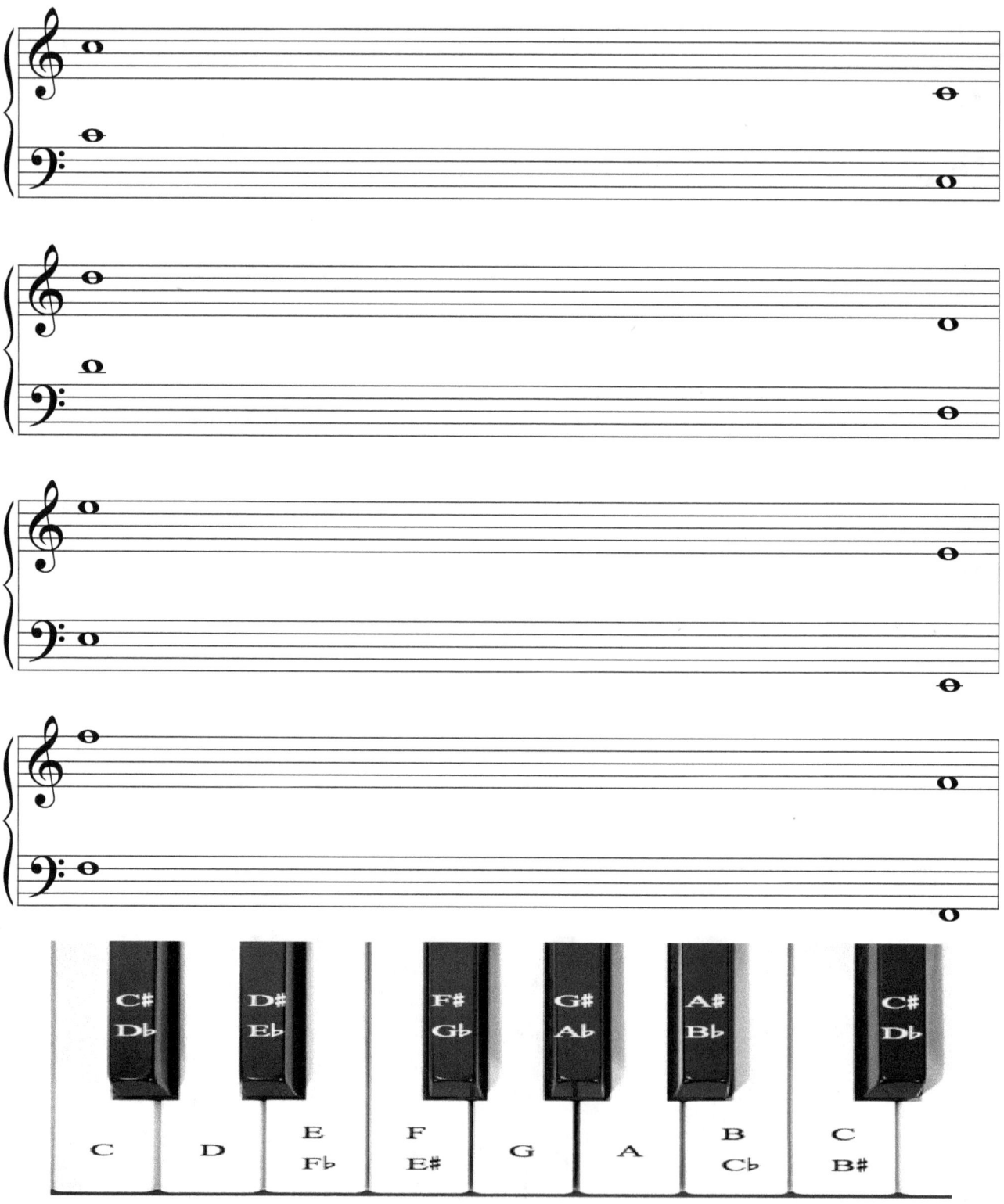

3. *Draw an ascending chromatic scale in the first measure and a descending chromatic scale in the second measure of each system. Use half notes.*

4. *Draw the enharmonic note after the given note. Then write the note names underneath the notes. Use whole notes. The first one is done for you.*

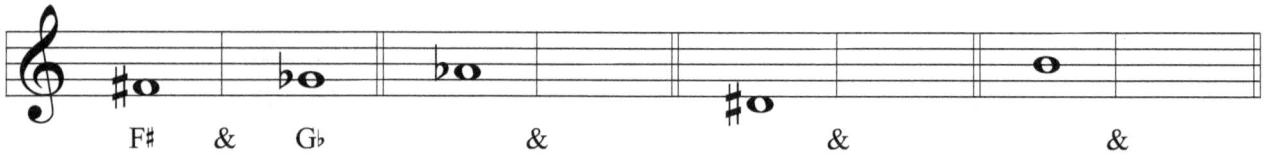

F♯ & G♭   & _____   & _____   & _____

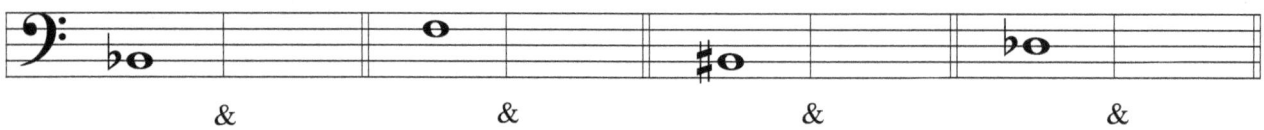

_____ & _____   & _____   & _____   & _____

5. *Name the enharmonic note after the given note. The first one is done for you.*

C♯ & D♭   F♯ & _____   E & _____   A♭ & _____   G♯ & _____   B♭ & _____

E♭ & _____   A♯ & _____   F♭ & _____   B♯ & _____   E♯ & _____   D♭ & _____

6. *Fill in the missing enharmonic note names on the keyboard. If you need help, you can refer to the keyboard on page 6.*

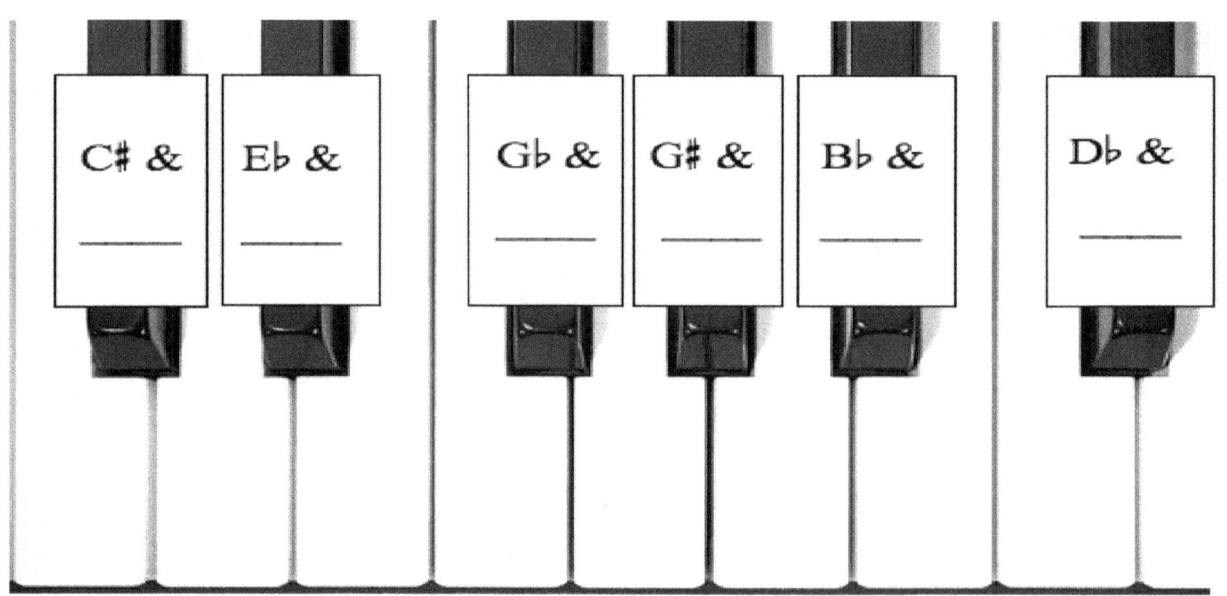

MUSIC THEORY FOR SINGERS

THE NATURAL MINOR SCALE

Every Major key has a "relative" minor key. The Major and relative minor key share the same key signature (sharps/flats). You can find the relative minor key by going to the 6th note of the Major Key's scale (in solfege, this is the "La") or by singing the note that is a minor third (3 half steps) lower than the Major Key's Do.

In the examples below, there are scales in a Major key and in its relative minor key. You'll notice that both the Major and minor keys have the same key signature (sharps/flats).

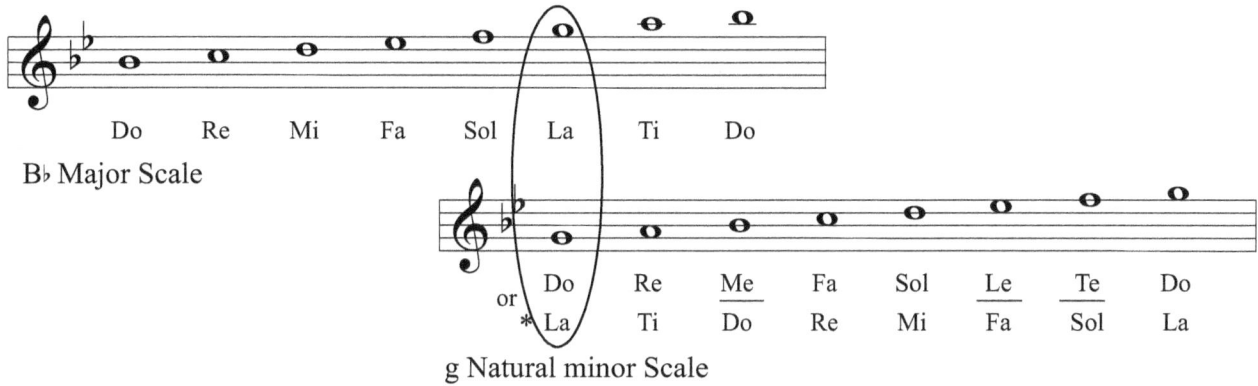

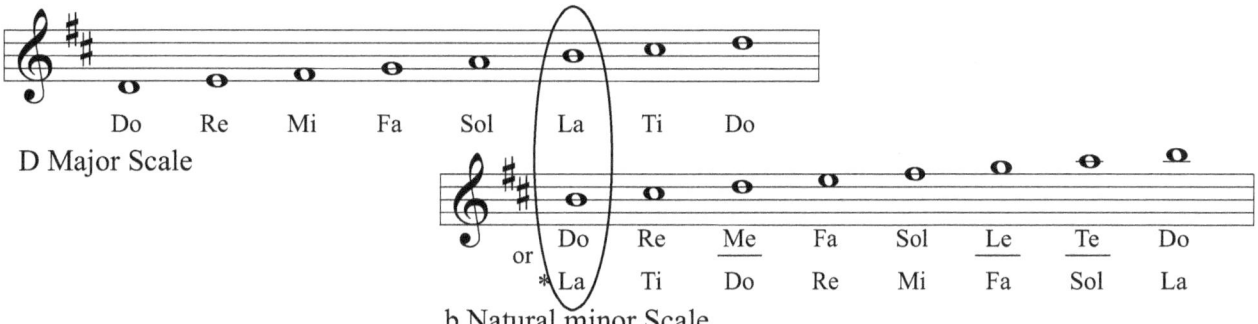

Note that the Do of the Relative Major Scale is the 3rd tone, "Me," of the minor scale.

There are three forms of a minor scale: Natural, Harmonic & Melodic. In this level, you will be introduced to the Natural minor scale. A minor scale in its "Natural" state is simply a minor scale that shares the same sharps/flats with it's relative Major key.

When singing a Natural minor scale, the solfege is slightly different. The 3rd, 6th & 7th notes are lowered, so the solfege changes. The altered solfege represents the different notes and sounds that are in a minor scale.

Solfege for an ascending minor scale is: Do-Re-Me-Fa-Sol-Le-Te- Do.

*Another way to sing the solfege is with the relative Major key in mind. The minor scale starts on the La of the relative Major scale. The pitches are the same, but the solfege is La-Ti-Do-Re-Mi-Fa-Sol-La.

MUSIC THEORY FOR SINGERS

MINOR KEY SIGNATURES

Below are examples of new minor key signatures in this level. You will see the Major scales and their relative minor scales below.

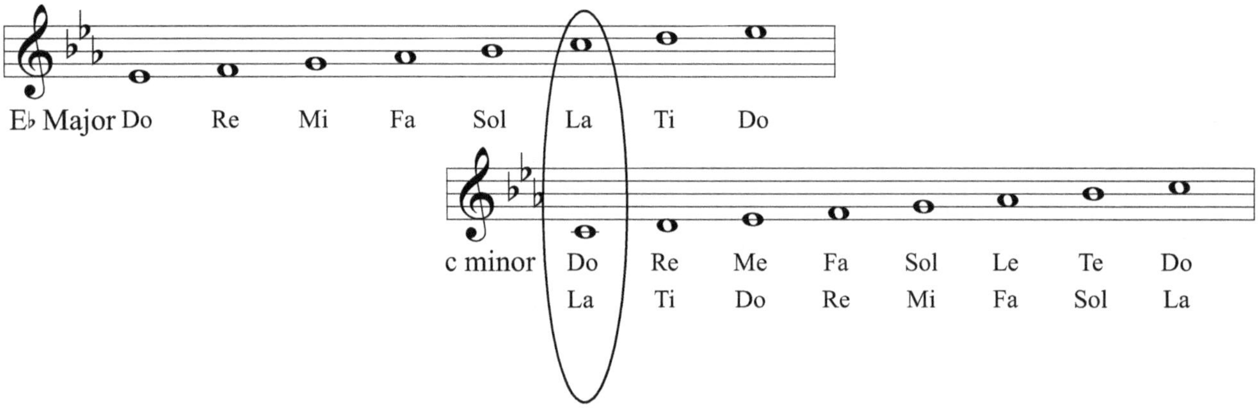

B Major — Do Re Mi Fa Sol La Ti Do

g# minor — Do Re Me Fa Sol Le Te Do
             La Ti Do Re Mi Fa Sol La

E♭ Major — Do Re Mi Fa Sol La Ti Do

c minor — Do Re Me Fa Sol Le Te Do
          La Ti Do Re Mi Fa Sol La

Remember, you can also count 3 notes (or 3 half steps) down to find the relative minor key.
f is 3 half steps lower than A♭, so it is the relative minor key.

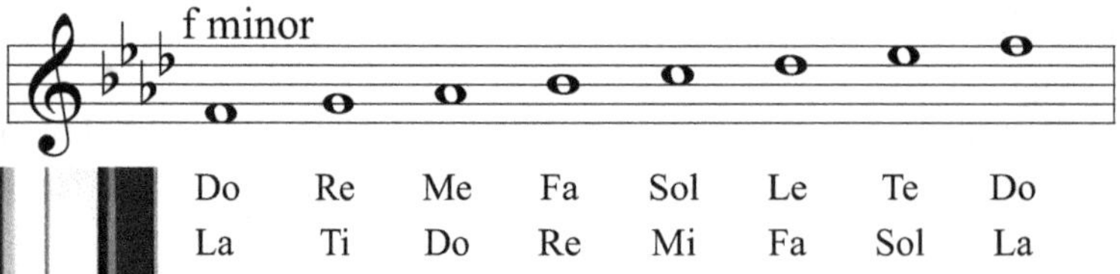

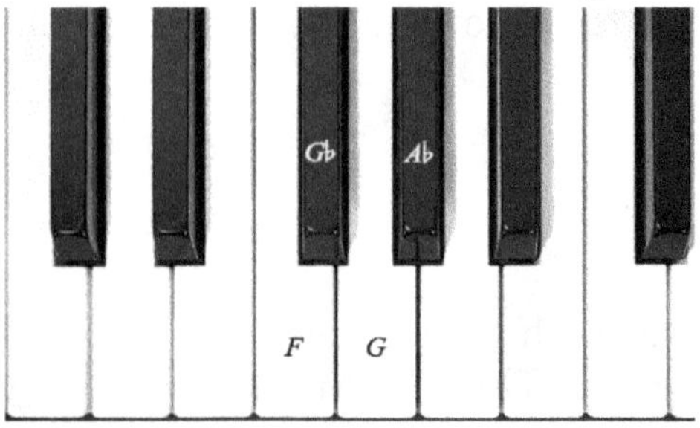

A♭ Major — Do Re Mi Fa Sol La Ti Do

f minor — Do Re Me Fa Sol Le Te Do
          La Ti Do Re Mi Fa Sol La

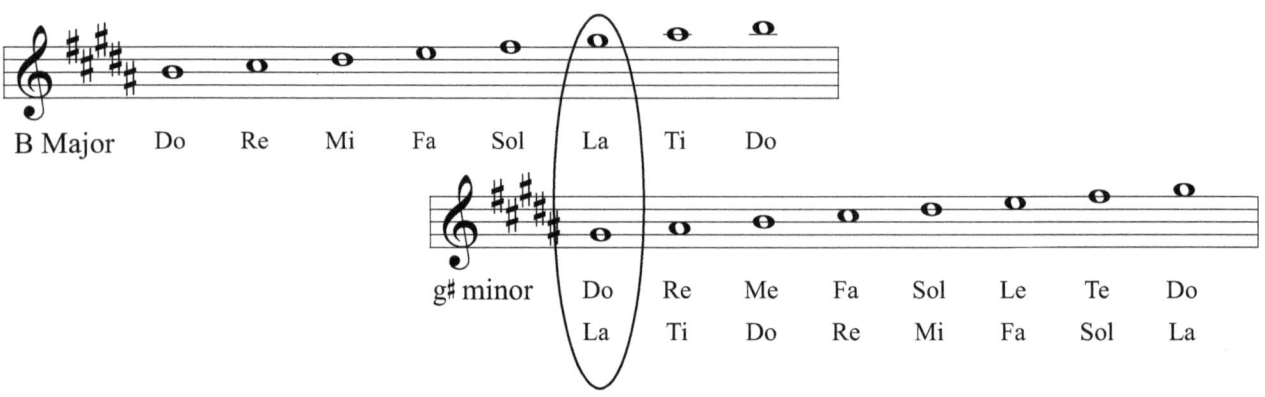

MUSIC THEORY FOR SINGERS

MINOR TRIADS

A <u>Triad</u>, or 3-note chord, is formed when the first, third and fifth notes of a scale are sung or played either consecutively or at the same time. The root, or the lowest note of a triad, gives it its letter name. Example: c minor.

The following examples show the minor scales and minor triads formed on the first note of the scale (Do).

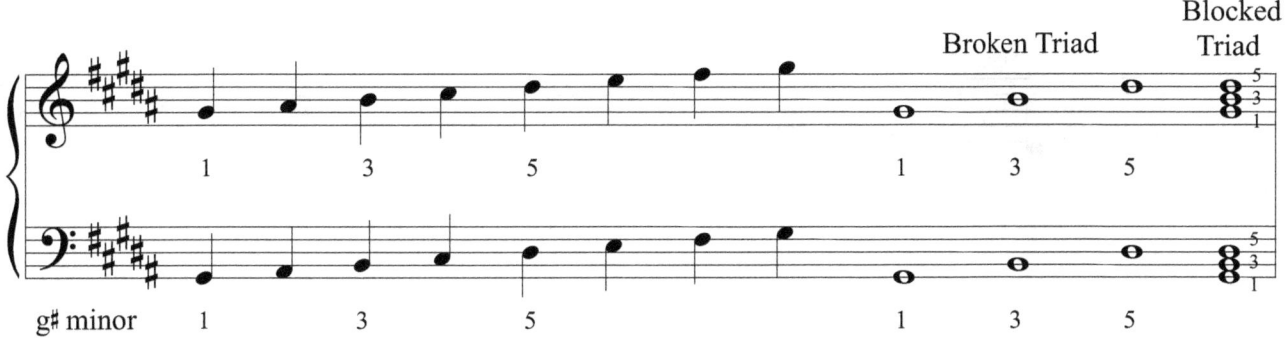

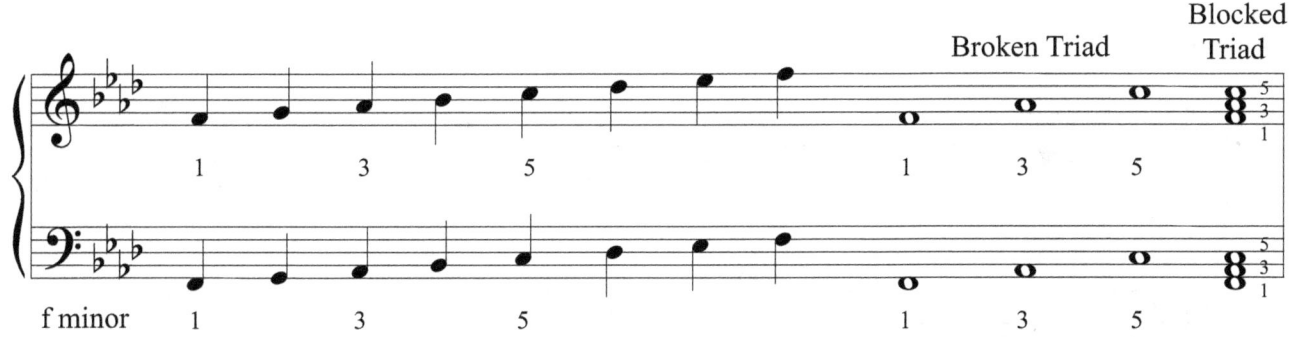

REVIEW: NATURAL MINOR SCALES & TRIADS

1. *Add the missing sharps or flats to create natural minor scales. <u>Do not use a key signature.</u> Remember, think about the relative Major key, which you can find by counting up 3 half steps. You can also go to the third note of the minor scale, "me," which happens to be "do" in the relative Major scale This will help you find how many sharps or flats are in the key signature.*

2. *Draw the correct key signature after the treble and bass clefs, then draw a blocked triad on Do on both the treble and bass staves. Use half notes.*

g♯ minor   c minor   f minor

3. *Draw the correct key signature after the treble and bass clefs.*
Draw an ascending Natural minor scale in the first measure and a descending scale in the second measure in both the treble and bass clefs, using quarter notes.
Remember, you don't have to add ♮/♭ to the scale once you have a key signature.

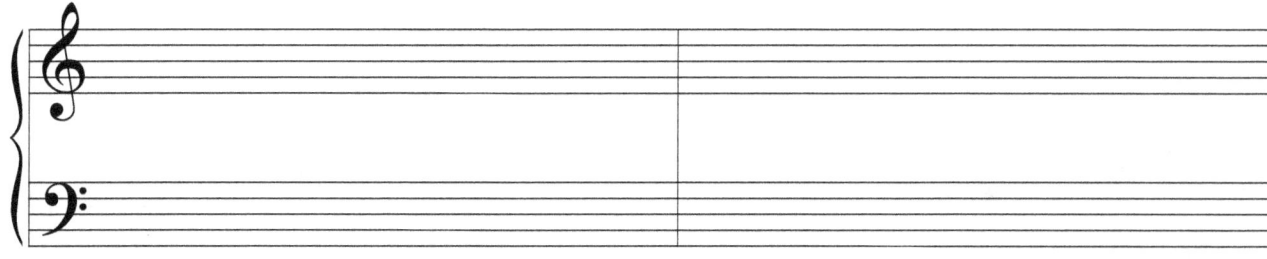

g♯ minor

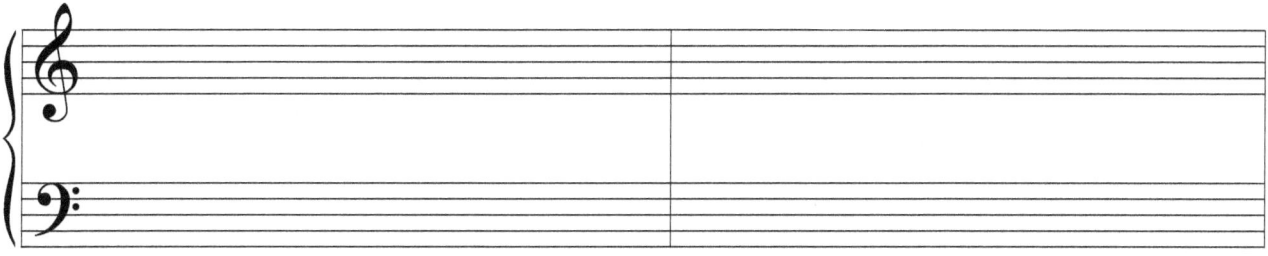

c minor

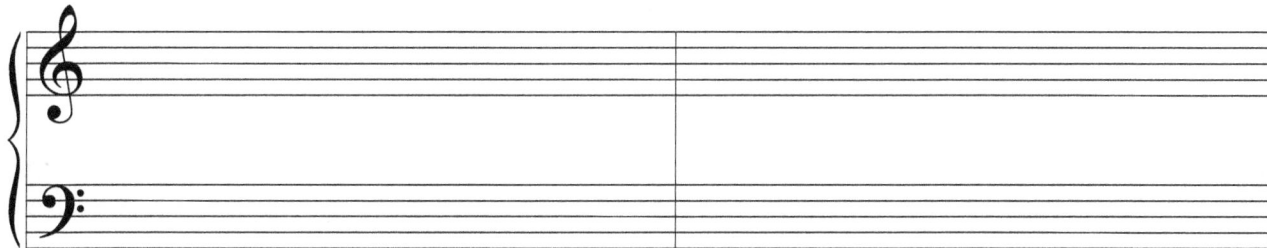

f minor

4. *For the following examples:*
- *Circle the notes affected by the key signature.*
- *Write the note names underneath the notes. Be sure to add the ♯ or ♭ if indicated by the key signature.*
- *Don't forget to add the ♯ or ♭ AFTER the letter name of the notes. (F♯, B♭...)*

Make sure you pay attention to the clefs!!

THE APPOGGIATURA, MORDENT & GRACE NOTE

The Appoggiatura: This is an accented, non-harmonic note that resolves stepwise to a harmonic note, often written in small type.

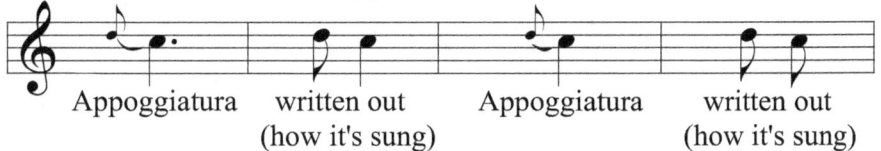

(The Appoggiatura always gets its full value, and this value is subtracted from the note of resolution).

The Mordent: This is an ornament where the main note and the note below are sung quickly in succession before returning to the main note.

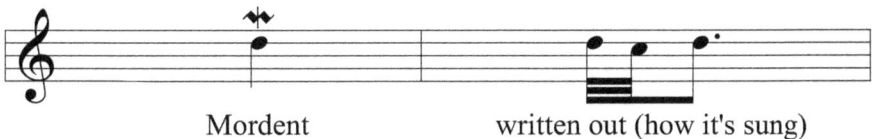

The Grace Note: This is an unaccented ornament consisting of a short note immediately before a longer-lasting note. Grace notes are written in small type, with a slash through the stem.

Here's an example of each ornament within a piece of music...

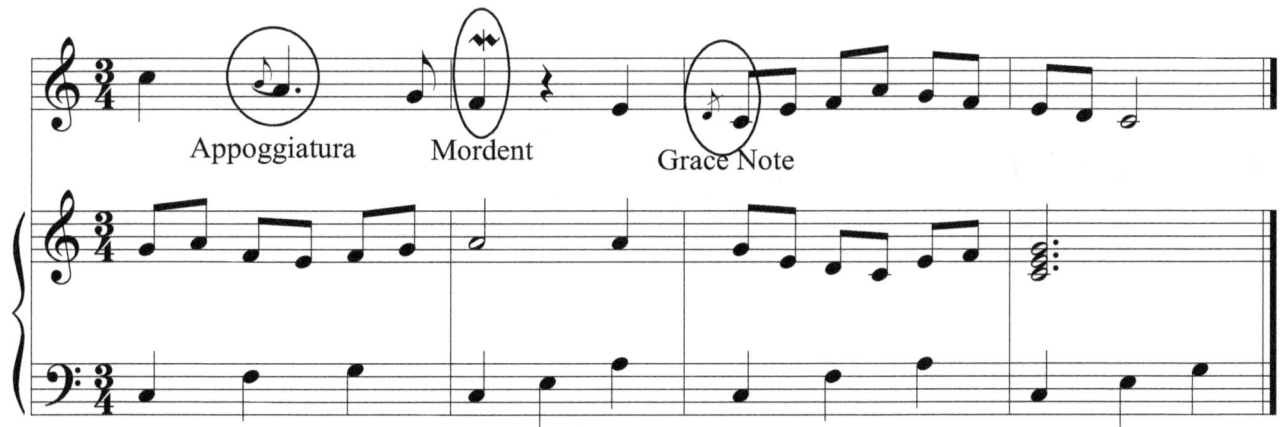

MUSIC THEORY FOR SINGERS

RHYTHM

Below is a review of rhythms in various time signatures. The beats have been written under the notes/rests as well as "La" to show you how to sing these rhythms.

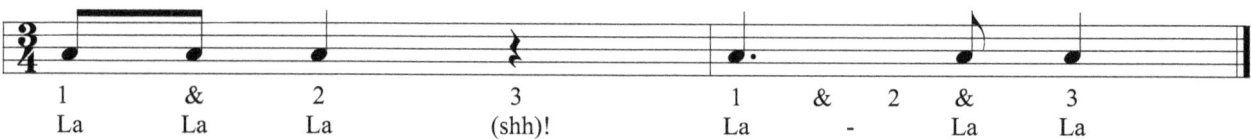

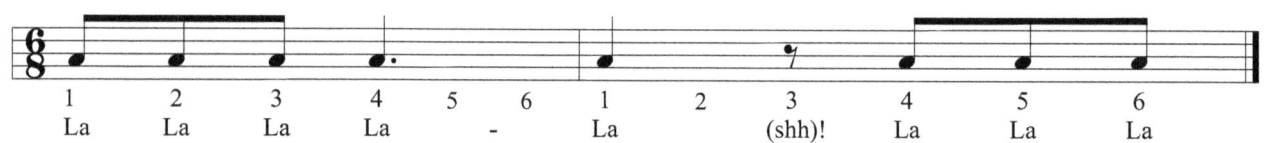

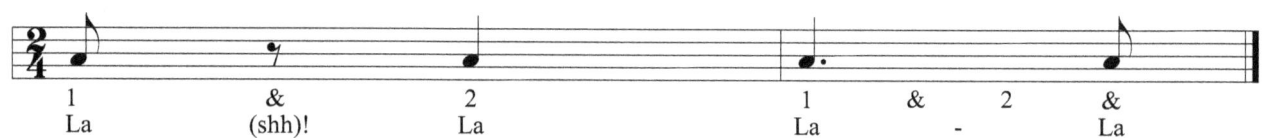

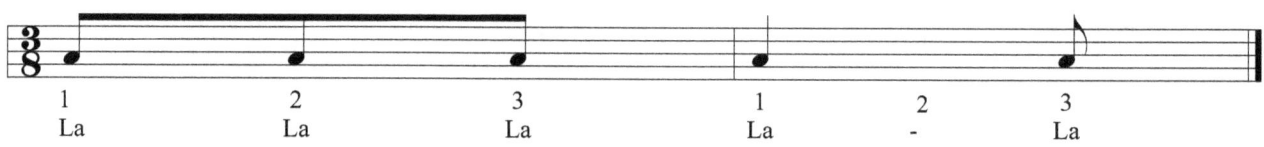

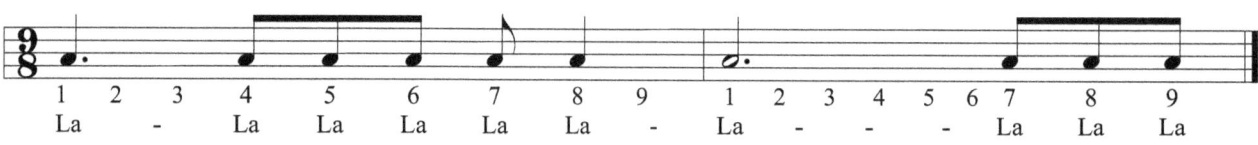

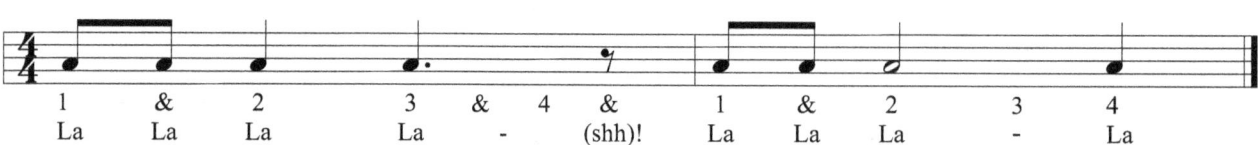

REVIEW: APPOGGIATURA, MORDENT, GRACE NOTE & RHYTHM

1. *Draw a line connecting the ornament on the left to it's correct written out version on the right.*

2. *Write the name under each ornament in the following musical example: Appoggiatura, Mordent & Grace Note.*

3. *Write the beats underneath the notes/rests in each example. Then add the three missing bar lines and a double bar line. Then practice singing each example on "La."*

4. *Add one missing note or rest to each measure. Practice singing each example on "La."*

5. *Fill in the missing time signature for each example. Then, write the beats under the notes/rests. Try singing the examples on "La."*

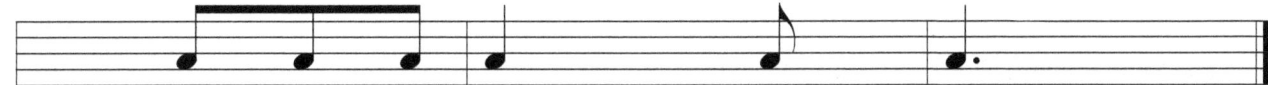

MAJOR CHORD PROGRESSIONS

A <u>Chord Progression</u> is a series of chords that helps to establish tonality within a song. For singers, chord progressions can usually be found in the piano accompaniment, or in the vocal line within a choral piece. In this level, you will learn about the most commonly found chord progression:

I - IV - V - I

Remember, the Tonic chord (I) consists of the Root, 3rd and 5th notes of the Major Scale, and is a Major triad.

The Subdominant chord (IV) is a Major triad built on the 4th note of the Major Scale.

The Dominant chord (V) is a Major triad built on the 5th note of the Major Scale.

Look at the examples below in C Major.

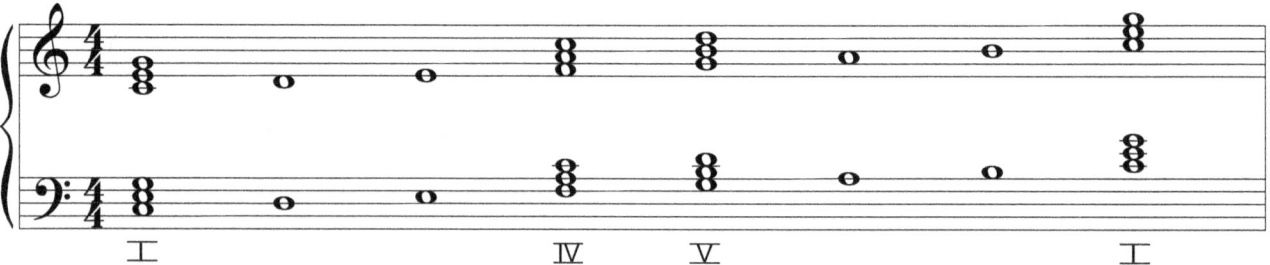

Chord progressions are often found in 1st and 2nd inversions. In level 6, you learned that an inversion of a chord is simply rearranging the notes in a different order, like juggling. The three notes in the triad do not change, just their order does. Typically, the IV chord is found in 2nd inversion, while the V chord is found in 1st inversion. The I chord is usually found in Root Position. Keep in mind that chords can be in any inversion; the order of the notes doesn't matter, just the notes themselves.

Below is a musical example with a chord progression in the accompaniment.

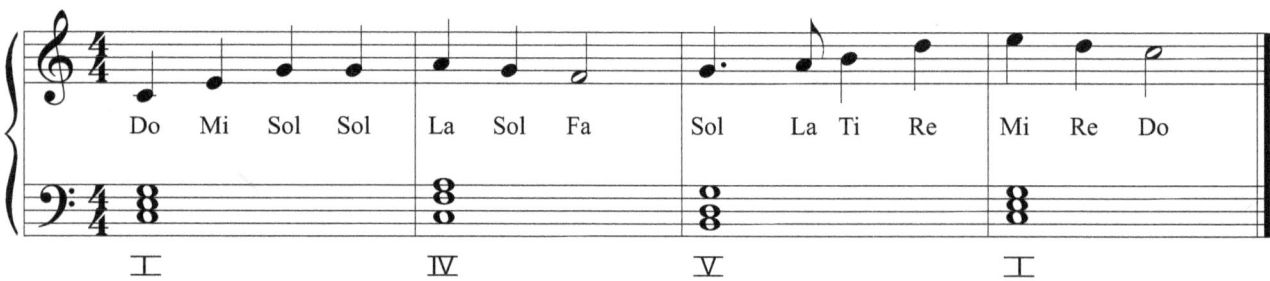

MUSIC THEORY FOR SINGERS

THE V AND V7 CHORDS

The dominant triad (3-note chord) is a Major triad, built on the 5th note of a Major Scale. A dominant 7th chord is a chord built on the dominant (5th note of a Major scale) containing a Major triad and an added minor seventh (for example: G-B-D-F in C Major). The dominant 7th chord or V 7 is the most commonly heard version of a V chord in music. It is usually written in an inversion, but both the root and inversion are notated below.

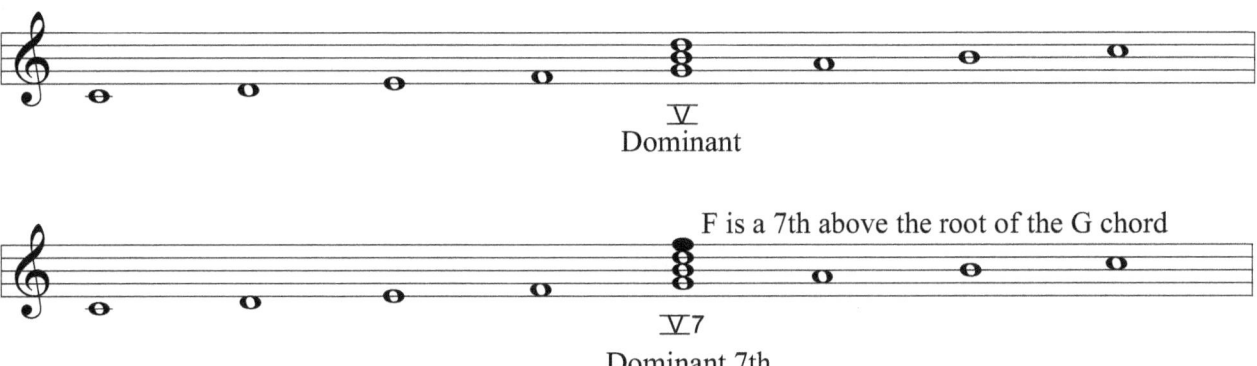

Here is a Root position Dominant and Dominant 7th chord in the key of D Major

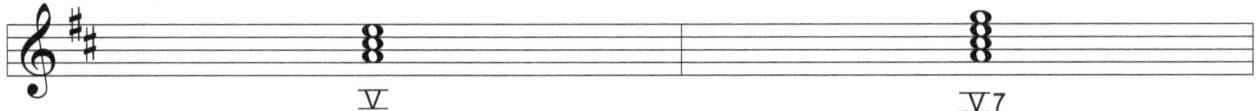

INVERSIONS OF DOMINANT 7TH CHORDS

Dominant 7th chords have three inversions because there are 4 notes. Look at the example below. Follow the Root (G) for each of the inversions.

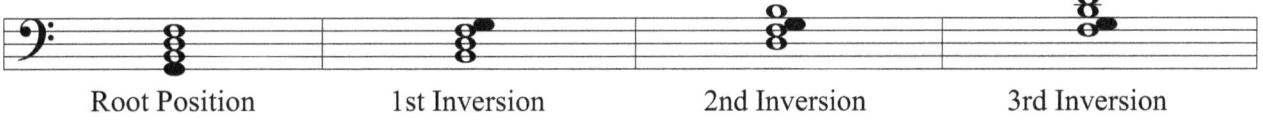

In chord progressions, the 1st inversion of the Dominant 7th chord is typically used, and the 5th is often omitted. Since the 5th note is the same in Major and minor keys, removing it doesn't change the quality.

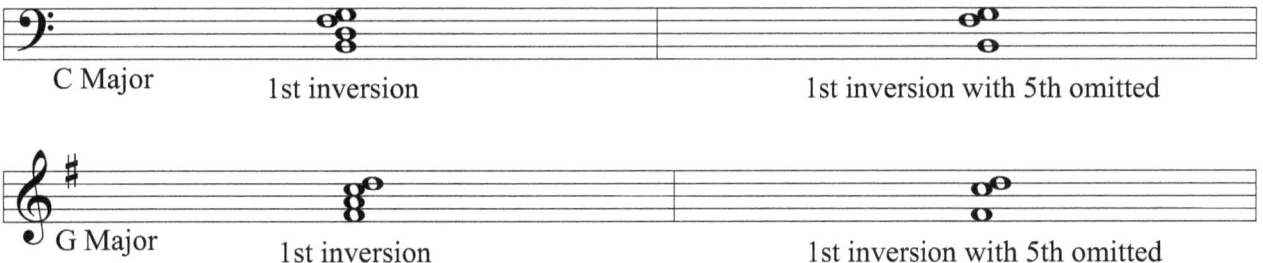

MUSIC THEORY FOR SINGERS

MAJOR & MINOR CHORD PROGRESSIONS

In the chord progression I - IV - V7 - I, the V7 chord is typically Major in both Major and minor keys. Look at the following examples in the key of C Major and c minor.

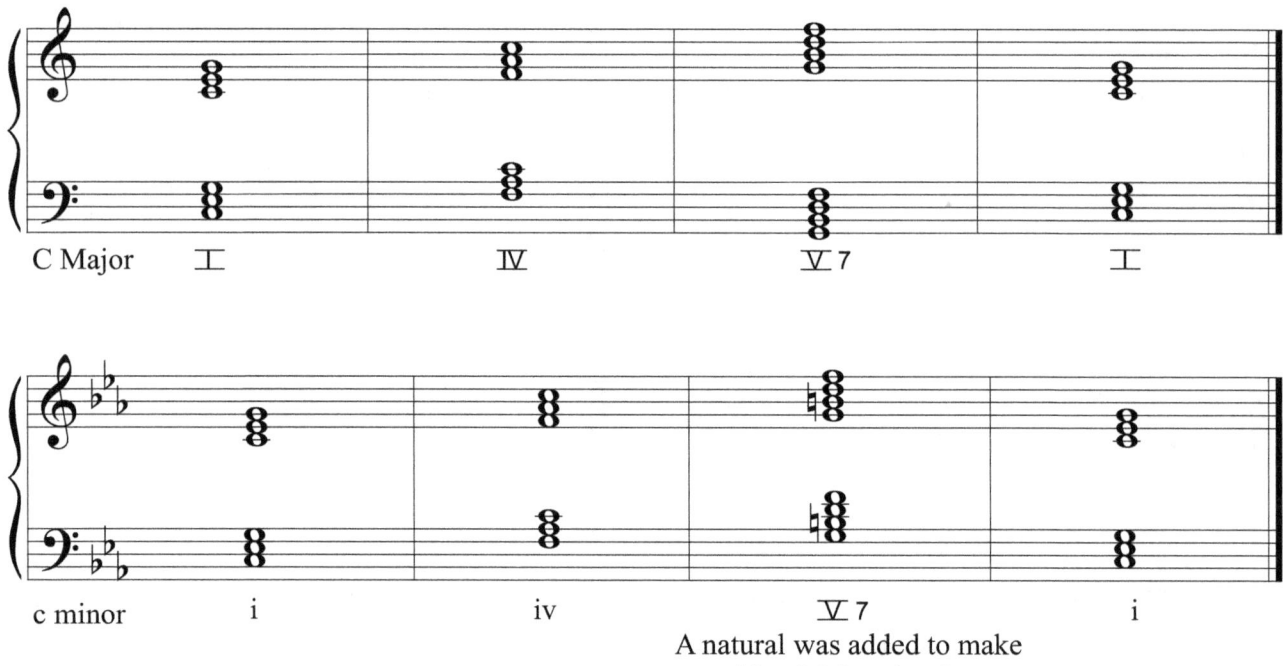

A natural was added to make this a Major chord.

Here are some chord progressions in other Major and minor keys...

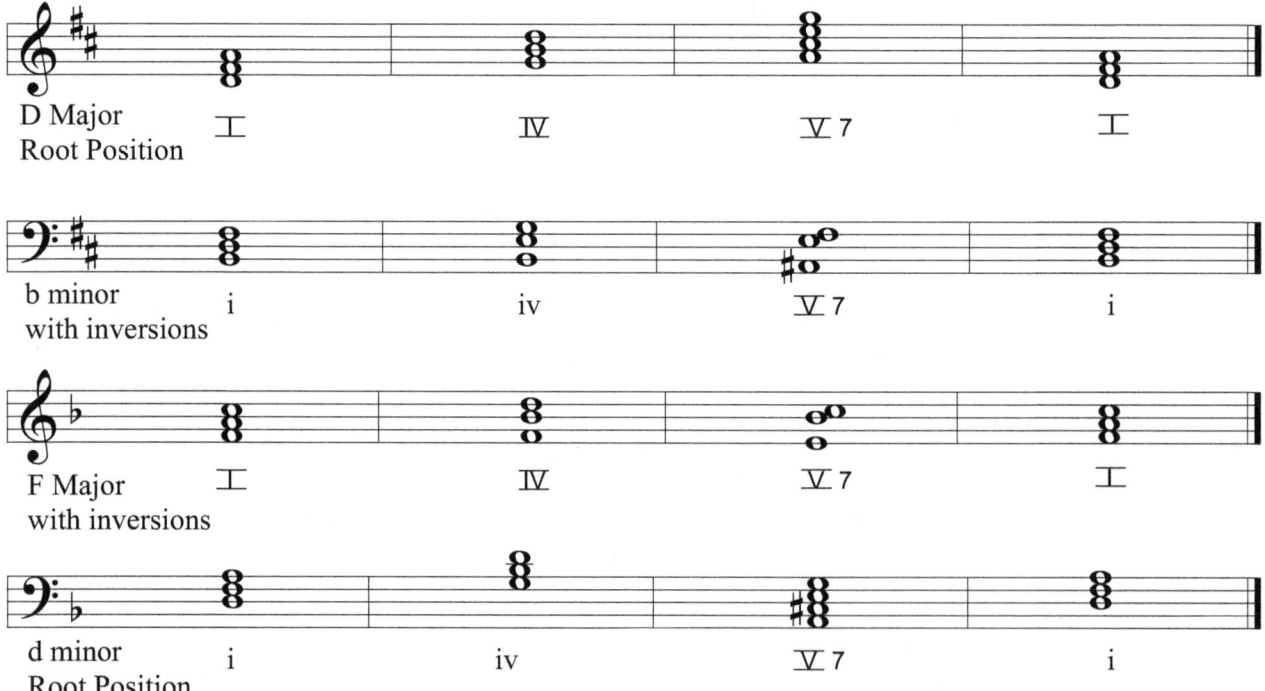

CADENCES: AUTHENTIC, PLAGAL & HALF

In music, a cadence is a progression of at least two chords that ends a phrase, section, or piece of music. The most common cadences are the Authentic, Plagal and Half Cadences.

Authentic Cadence: V - I or V7 - I

Plagal Cadence: IV - I

Half Cadence: I - V / V7, or IV - V / V7

When a phrase, section or piece of music ends on the Tonic chord (I), it sounds final, or complete. A Half Cadence ends on the V, so it sounds incomplete. One way to remember the Half Cadence is that it's "Half-done" or "Half-over."

Below are examples of Authentic, Plagal and Half Cadences in the key of D Major. You will see examples of both Root position and inversions.

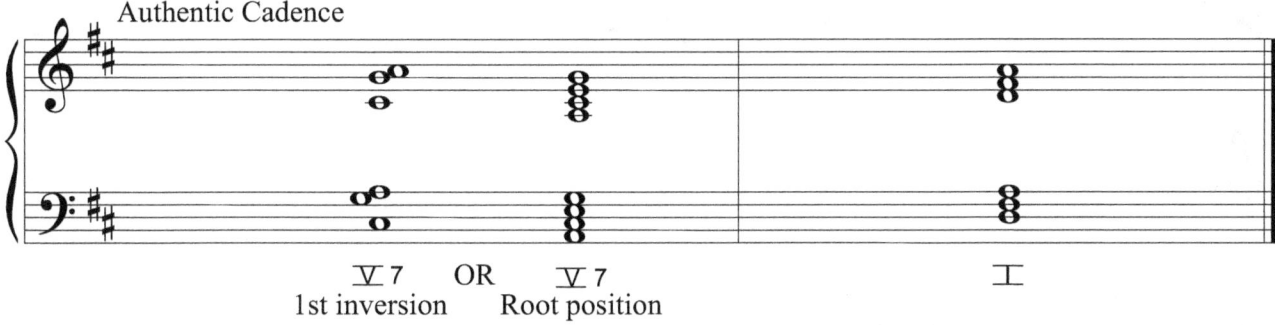

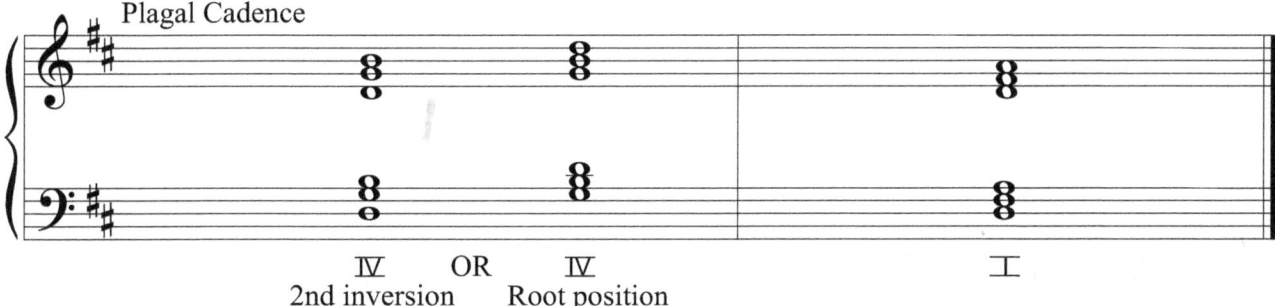

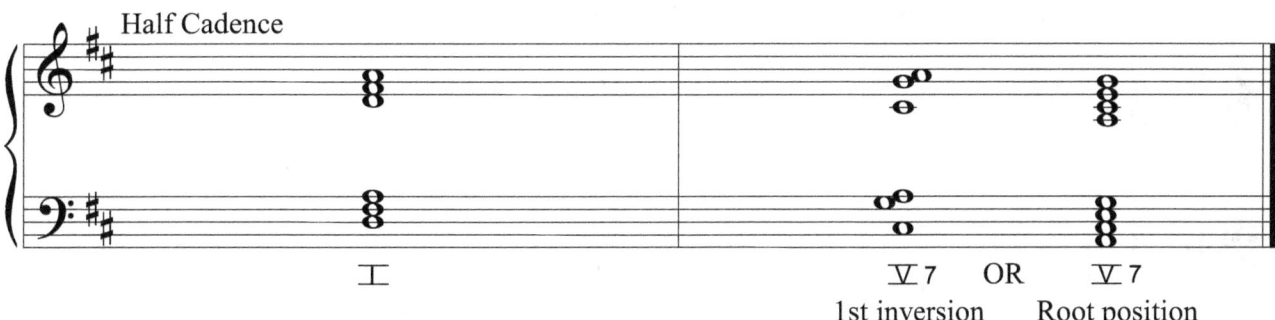

MUSIC THEORY FOR SINGERS

This musical example has Major chord progressions and an Authentic Cadence.

This musical example has minor chord progressions and a Plagal Cadence.

This musical example has Major chord progressions and a Half Cadence.

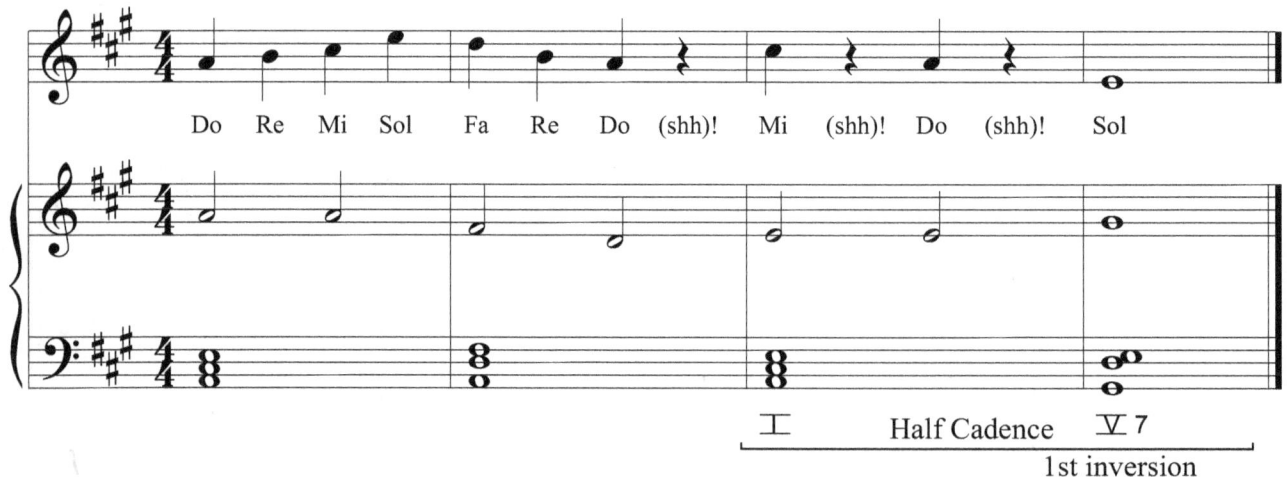

REVIEW: CHORD PROGRESSIONS & CADENCES

1. *Label the following chords with the correct name and Roman Numeral. Each example has a Tonic, Subdominant, Dominant & Tonic Chord. Some Dominant chords are Dominant 7th chords. Remember to use lower case Roman Numerals for the Tonic & Subdominant in minor keys. Some examples are in Root position and some are in inversions. The first one is done for you.*

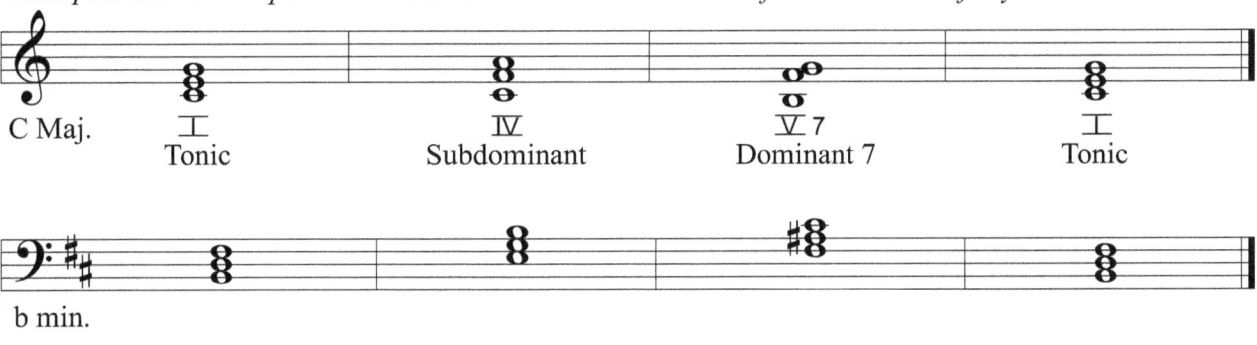

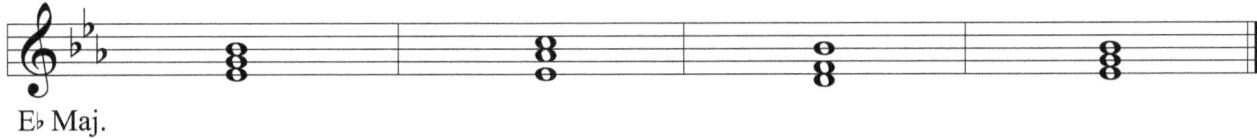

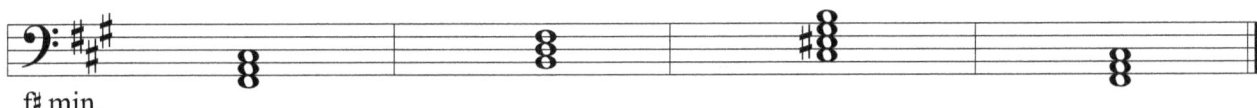

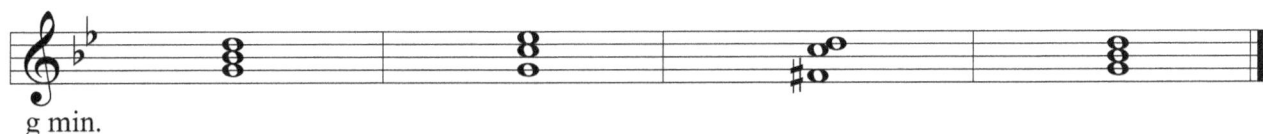

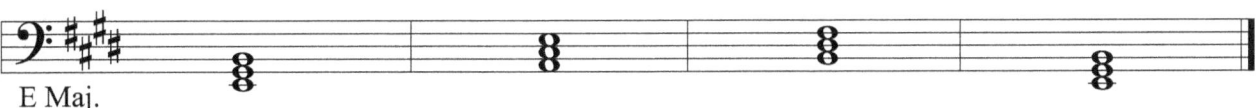

2. *Draw Tonic, Subdominant & Dominant 7th chords in the following Major and minor keys. Use either all Root position chords, or try to use the inversions of the IV and V7 chords for some examples. Look on pages 20-21 if you need help with the inversions.*
Label each chord with the correct Roman numerals.

3. *Write the correct Roman Numerals under the chords then label each cadence as "Authentic," "Plagal," or "Half." Note that some chords are in inversions and some are in Root position.*

4. *Look at the following musical examples and label the cadence in the last two measures.*

_____ Cadence

_____ Cadence

_____ Cadence

FEMALE VOICE CLASSIFICATIONS

It's important for you, as a singer, to understand your voice type. Voice type depends on many factors including the length and width of your vocal cords. Voice types also change over time, especially during adolescence.

Below is a description of the most common female voice types and their approximate ranges. They are listed in order from highest voice type to lowest voice type. Specific ranges vary from person to person (C4 = Middle C).

Coloratura Soprano -a type of operatic soprano voice who specializes in music with leaps, runs and trills.

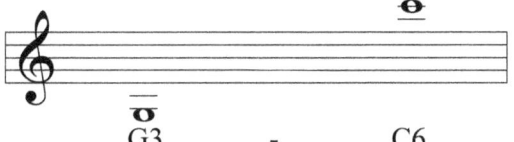

G3 - C6

Lyric Soprano -a very agile, light voice with a high range, capable of very fast coloratura; bel canto roles were written for this voice.

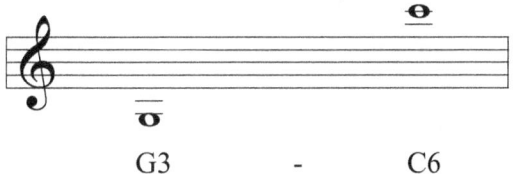

G3 - C6

Dramatic Soprano -a coloratura soprano of great flexibility in high velocity passages, with great sustaining power.

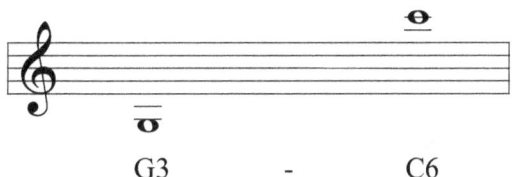

G3 - C6

Mezzo-Soprano -means "middle" soprano, with a darker color and the ability to extend the range.

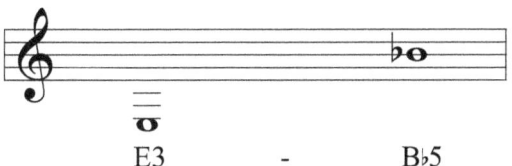

E3 - B♭5

Contralto (alto) - is the deepest female classical voice, falling between tenor and mezzo-soprano.

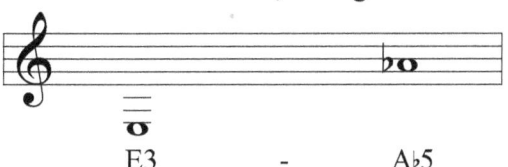

E3 - A♭5

MALE VOICE CLASSIFICATIONS

Below is a description of the most common male voice types and their approximate ranges. They are listed in order from highest voice type to lowest voice type. Specific ranges vary from person to person (C4 = Middle C).

Countertenor- a male singing voice whose vocal range is equivalent to a contralto, mezzo-soprano or soprano.

C3 - E5

Lyric Tenor- a light, agile tenor with the ability to sing difficult passages of high velocity.

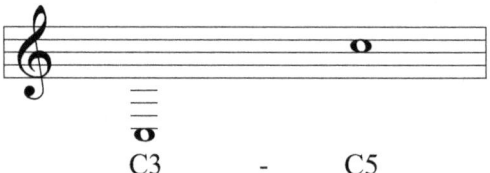
C3 - C5

Dramatic Tenor- a tenor with the brightness and height of a lyric tenor but a heavier vocal weight which can be "pushed" to dramatic climaxes.

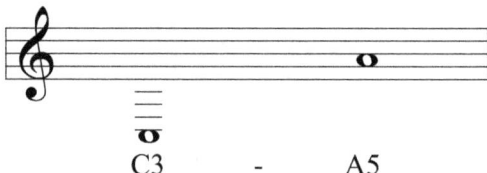
C3 - A5

Baritone- a type of male singing voice that lies between bass and tenor voices; the most common male voice.

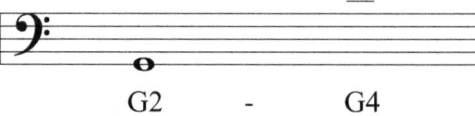
G2 - G4

Bass/Baritone- a voice that is richer and fuller and sometimes harsh, with a darker quality.

G2 - F4

Bass (Basso Profundo)- a deep, heavy bass voice with an exceptionally low range; the lowest bass voice type.

E2 - E4

MUSIC THEORY FOR SINGERS

RHYTHMIC SIGHT-SINGING

In order to learn a song, singers learn to read rhythmic patterns and notes on the staff. Singing a melody for the first time is called "Sight-singing." Below are some examples of rhythmic patterns in 6/8 time, that contain a variety of notes and rests.

Hint: When singing rhythmic examples, take a breath on the rests: then you won't miss them! Tap and say the beats, then sing the examples on a La (choose any pitch that suits your voice).

SIGHT-SINGING & SOLFEGE: NATURAL MINOR

<u>Solfege</u> is a system of assigning a syllable to each note of a scale, just like in the song "Do-Re-Mi" from the musical *The Sound of Music*.
Solfege is what you use when sight-singing. Moveable "Do" is when "Do" matches whatever key you're in.

In this level you will be introduced to melodies in a natural minor key, in the range of an octave. When singing a Natural minor scale, the solfege is slightly different. The 3rd, 6th & 7th notes are lowered, so the solfege changes. The altered solfege represents the different notes and sounds that are in a minor scale.

Solfege for an ascending minor scale is: Do-Re-<u>Me</u>-Fa-Sol-<u>Le</u>-<u>Te</u>- Do. You may also use the solfege that relates to the relative Major key: La-Ti-Do-Re-Mi-Fa-Sol-La. The following melodies are all minor.

(Me is pronounced "May," Le is pronounced "Lay," Te is pronounced "Tay.")

MUSIC THEORY FOR SINGERS

REVIEW: VOICE CLASSIFICATIONS & SIGHT-SINGING

1. *Match the following voice classifications with their definitions. F=Female, M=Male.*

a. Coloratura Soprano _____ (F) a very agile, light voice with a high range, capable of very fast coloratura; bel canto roles were written for this voice.

b. Lyric Soprano _____ (M) a light, agile tenor with ability to sing difficult passages of high velocity.

c. Dramatic Soprano _____ (M) a deep, heavy bass voice with an exceptionally low range, the lowest bass voice type.

d. Mezzo Soprano _____ (M) a tenor with the brightness and height of a lyric tenor but a heavier vocal weight which can be "pushed" to dramatic climaxes.

e. Contralto (alto) _____ (F) a type of operatic soprano voice who specializes in music with leaps, runs and trills.

f. Countertenor _____ (M) a type of male singing voice that lies between bass and tenor voices-the most common male voice.

g. Lyric Tenor _____ (F) meaning "middle" soprano, with a darker color and ability to exten the range.

h. Dramatic Tenor _____ (M) a voice that is richer and fuller and sometimes harsh, with a darker quality.

i. Baritone _____ (F) the deepest female classical voice, falling between tenor and mezzo-soprano.

j. Bass/Baritone _____ (M) a male singing voice whose vocal range is equivalent to a contralto, mezzo soprano or soprano.

k. Bass (Basso Profundo) _____ (F) a coloratura soprano of great flexibility in high velocity passages, with great sustaining power.

MUSIC THEORY FOR SINGERS

2. *Write the beats under the following examples, then try singing them on a "La."*

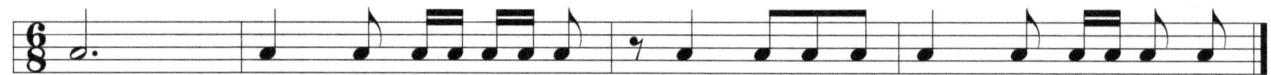

3. *For the following melodies, write the note names and solfege underneath the notes. Pay attention to the key signatures (Major or minor). Add ♯/♭ when necessary. Try singing the examples when you are done!*

d min.

Note Names: _____

Solfege: _____

c min.

Note Names: _____

Solfege: _____

F Maj.

Note Names: _____

Solfege: _____

A Maj.

Note Names: _____

Solfege: _____

b min.

Note Names: _____

Solfege: _____

e min.

Note Names: _____

Solfege: _____

4. *Practice the following melodies:*
Tap and say the beats.
Sing melodies on Solfege or note names while tapping the beat.
All Major melodies start on "Do." For minor melodies, you may start on "Do" (with altered solfege) or start on "La" with the relative Major key in mind.

D Maj.

B♭ Maj.

b min.

c min.

d min.

c♯ min.

MUSICAL TERMS

A crucial part of understanding music is being able to recognize and define musical terms. Below is a list of terms covered in this level with some additional ones.

animé - (Fr.) moderately fast, animated

appoggiatura - (♪♩) an accented, non-harmonic note that resolves stepwise to a harmonic note, often written in small type but receiving its full value, taken from the note of resolution

aria - a song for solo voice within an opera or oratorio

cadence - the series of notes or chords that ends a melody or section, giving the listener a sense of finality

cadenza - a solo passage, often technically difficult, usually near the end of a piece, either written by the composer or improvised by the performer

chanson - (Fr.) song

chromatic - moving by half steps

doucement - (Fr.) gently, softly

enharmonic - two notes that have the same pitch but different names

imitation - a compositional technique consisting of the overlapping repetition of a melody by two or more "voices"

léger - (Fr.) light and fast

lentement - (Fr.) slowly

libretto - the text, whether spoken or sung, of a dramatic vocal work

misterioso - mysteriously

modéré - (Fr.) moderately

mordent - (♩) an ornament where the main note and the note below are sung quickly in succession before returning to the main note.

portamento - a smooth glide from one note to another

recitative - a vocal number that mimics the inflections of speech, found primarily in operas & oratorios

rubato - freely speeding up or slowing down the tempo without changing the basic beat

triste - (Fr.) sad

vite - (Fr.) fast

MUSIC THEORY FOR SINGERS

SPOTLIGHT ON COMPOSERS

An important part of music education is learning about the history of music. Studying composers allows for understanding the music we sing and why it was written the way it was. In this level, you will learn about Enrique Granados, Gabriel Fauré & Aaron Copland.

ENRIQUE GRANADOS

Enrique Granados was born in the Late Romantic/Impressionist period of music, on July 27, 1867 in Lleida, Spain. He studied piano in Barcelona and Paris when he was young. He published his Danzas Españolas in 1889, which brought him international recognition.

Granados gave many concerts in Spain, France and New York. He wrote chamber music, vocal music, operas, symphonic poems and piano works. In 1898, Granados premiered his first zarzuela (Spanish opera) *Maria del Carmen*. A zarzuela is a Spanish Opera with alternating spoken and sung scenes.

In 1901, Granados founded the Academia Granados in Barcelona, Spain. Many famous musicians came out of this academy including Paquita Madriguera, Conchita Badia and Frank Marshall. In 1916, Granados's opera *Goyescas* (a piano suite converted into an opera) premeiered at the Metropolitan Opera in New York. In this same year, he also performed at the White House for president Woodrow Wilson.

Tragically, on March 24, 1916, Granados and his wife were traveling across the English Channel, (Granados was terrified of the water), when a German torpedo hit the boat. Granados tried to save his wife, but they both drowned. They left six children.

Best Known Vocal Works:
Maria del Carmen (1898-Opera), *Goyescas* (1916-Opera), *Tonadillas al estilo antiguo* (for voice and piano), *Canciones Españolas* (for voice and piano)

Vocal Songs:
"El Majo Discreto," "La Maja Dolorosa," "El mirar de la Maja," "El tra-la-la y el Punteado"

GABRIEL FAURÉ

Gabriel Fauré was born in the Late Romantic/Impressionist/ Early 20th Century period of music on May 12, 1845 in France. As a child, he was a gifted pianist and was sent to the École de Musique Classique et Religieuse (School of Classical and Religious Music) in Paris. During the 11 years at the school, he studied with such famous musicians as Niedermeyer, and Camille Saint-Saëns, who became a life-long friend.

After leaving the school, Fauré became the organist at the Church of Saint-Sauveur in Brittany and also gave private piano and organ lessons (his two main performance instruments). He also served in the military for a brief time before he was appointed choirmaster at the Église Saint-Sulpice. He also attended Saint-Saëns musical salon gatherings, joining the Société Nationale de Musique. Other members of this famous Society were Georges Bizet, Henri Duparc, César Franck, and Jules Massenet. Many of his works were first heard at the society's concerts.

Gabriel Faure: © Michael Nicholson/CORBIS

In 1877, Fauré was briefly engaged to Marianne Viardot, then he traveled a great deal to Germany, seeing several of Wagner's operas. Fauré married Marie Fremiet in 1883, and they had two sons. He did have several open relationships with other women, including the pianist Marguerite Hasselmans. In 1896, Fauré was appointed professor of composition at the Paris Conservatoire. He taught many young composers including Maurice Ravel, Louis Aubert and Nadia Boulanger. In 1905, he became the head of the Paris Conservatoire which helped him become more widely known as a composer. During this time, he wrote his lyric opera, *Pénélope*, and several vocal song cycles including *La chanson d'Ève*.

In 1909, Fauré was elected to the Institut de France. His music became popular in several countries including Britain, Germany, Spain and Russia. He became known as the Master of the French Art song, or "Mélodie." In 1911, he began to lose his hearing, which eventually forced him to leave his teaching position. In 1922, there was a public tribute in his honor in Sorbonne. He watched a concert of his own works, which made him very happy. He died in Paris from pneumonia on November 4th, 1924. He was 79 years old.

Best Known Vocal Works:
Requiem, *Op.48 (1888)*, **Pénélope** *(opera 1913)*, **La Bonne Chanson** *(song cycle)*, **Cinq mélodies de Venise** *(song cycle)*, **La chanson d'Ève** *(song cycle)*

Vocal Songs:
"Clair de lune," "Le Secret," "Nocturne," "Les présents," "Les berceaux," "Les roses d'Ispahan," "Après un rêve," "Au Bord de L'eau," "Mandoline," "Ici-bas"

AARON COPLAND

Aaron Copland: © Bettmann/CORBIS

Aaron Copland was born in the Contemporary period of music on November 14, 1900 in Brooklyn, New York. His sister, Laurine, first taught Aaron piano before he began formal lessons with Leopold Wolfsohn. He composed his first melody at the age of eleven and decided to become a composer by the time he was 15.

Copland studied piano (his main performance instrument), harmony, theory and composition from Rubin Goldmark, then studied later with Victor Wittgenstein. His most famous teacher in Paris was Nadia Boulanger. He studied with her for three years at the Paris Conservatory before returning to New York.

Around 1935, Copland began to compose music for young audiences including piano pieces and the opera *The Second Hurricane*. During the Depression, he traveled to Europe, Mexico and Africa and began writing one of his first famous works, *El Salón México*. In 1939, Copland finished his first two Hollywood film scores for *Of Mice and Men* & *Our Town*. He also wrote music for the ballet *Billy the Kid* that same year.

Copland became very active in the American Composers Alliance which helped collect fees pertaining to performance of composers copyrighted music. He also wrote the scores for the two ballets *Rodeo* & *Appalachian Spring* which were both successful. In 1942, he wrote the patriotic piece *Lincoln Portrait* for voice and orchestra which has become a patriotic standard along with his *Fanfare for the Common Man*.

In 1954, Copland recieved a commission from Rodgers and Hammerstein to write the music for the opera *The Tender Land*. This remains one of the few American operas in the standard repertory. Copland had a huge influence on other composers, including his friend Leonard Bernstein. When Copland was older he conducted more than composed, and he made a series of recordings.

Copland died of Alzheimer's disease and respiratory failure on December 2nd, 1990. He was 90 years old.

Best Known Vocal Works:
The Tender Land (Opera), ***The Second Hurricane*** (High School Opera), ***Twelve Poems by Emily Dickinson, Old American Songs, Canticle of Freedom***

Other Significant Works:
"The Cat and the Mouse," "Vocalise No.1" (Voice), ***Billy the Kid*** **(Ballet), "Fanfare for the Common Man," "Lincon Portrait"**

REVIEW: TERMS & COMPOSERS

1. *Fill in the correct answer using the terms from this level.*

a. An _____ is an accented, non-harmonic note that resolves stepwise to a harmonic note, often written in small type.

b. _____ means "song" in French.

c. The _____ is the text, whether spoken or sung, of a dramatic vocal work.

d. _____ means "slowly" in French.

e. A _____ is a smooth glide from one note to another.

f. A _____ is an ornament where the main note and the note below are sung quickly in succession before returning to the main note.

g. _____ means freely speeding up or slowing down the tempo without changing the basic beat.

h. _____ means "sad" in French.

i. A _____ is the series of notes or chords that ends a melody or section, giving the listener a sense of finality.

2. *Complete the following crossword puzzle using terms from this level.*

Level 7 Crossword

ACROSS

3 a vocal number that mimics the inflections of speech, found primarily in operas and oratorios
4 freely speeding up or slowing down the tempo without changing the basic beat
7 a solo passage, often technically difficult, usually near the end of a piece, either written by the composer or improvised by the performer
11 (Fr.) moderately
13 mysteriously
14 (Fr.) light and fast
17 (Fr.) sad
18 an ornament where the main note and the note below are sung quickly in succession before returning to the main note.
19 (Fr.) slowly
20 (Fr.) gently, softly

DOWN

1 the text, whether spoken or sung, of a dramatic vocal work
2 a song for solo voice within an opera or oratorio
5 (Fr.) moderately fast, animated
6 a compositional technique consisting of the overlapping repetition of a melody by two or more "voices"
7 (Fr.) song
8 an accented, non-harmonic note that resolves stepwise to a harmonic note, often written in small type
9 moving by half steps
10 two notes that have the same pitch but different names
12 a smooth glide from one note to another
15 (Fr.) fast
16 the series of notes or chords that ends a melody or section, giving the listener a sense of finality

MUSIC THEORY FOR SINGERS

3. *Fill in the correct answer to the following questions about Enrique Granados, Gabriel Fauré and Aaron Copland.*

Enrique Granados

a. Granados was born in which country?_____

b. What music period(s) does he represent?_____

c. What is the name of the music school he founded in Barcelona, Spain?_____

d. What is the name of his first opera?_____

e. What is a "Zarzuela?"_____

f. How did Granados die?_____.

Gabriel Fauré

a. Fauré was born in which country?_____

b. What music periods does he represent?_____

c. What are his two main performance instruments?_____

d. He is regarded as the master of what genre of vocal music?_____

e. In 1909, Fauré was elected to what institution?_____

f. What is the name of the French composer who taught Fauré and became a life-long friend?

_____

Aaron Copland

a. Copland was born in which country?_____

b. What music period does he represent?_____

c. What is the name of his famous female piano teacher from Paris?_____

d. Name his 1942 patriotic work written for voice and orchestra._____

e. Name Copland's two film scores that he completed in 1939._____ &

_____

f. What was Copland's main performance instrument?_____

MUSIC THEORY FOR SINGERS

LEVEL 7 REVIEW TEST

Answer the questions about the following musical example. (11 points)

1. What minor key is this song in? _____ minor

2. Define the term "Misterioso." _____

3. What type of cadence is in the Bass clef in measures 3-4? _____

4. What type of cadence is in the Bass clef in measures 7-8? _____
Note: the first chord is in first inversion.

5. How many times is this song sung? _____ once

   _____ twice

6. What type of ornament is in the vocal line in measure 1? _____

7. Write the solfege syllables for the circled section in m.6.

   _____ _____ _____ _____ _____

MUSIC THEORY FOR SINGERS

8. *Write an ascending and descending chromatic scale beginning and ending on middle C. (2 points, one for ascending, one for descending)*

9. *Write the enharmonic note after the given note for each example. (4 points)*

10. *Add 3 bar lines and a double bar line to the following example. (4 points)*

11. *Add the missing time signature, then write the beats underneath the notes. (5 points-one for the time signature, one for each correct measure)*

12. *Name, then draw the relative minor scale in its natural form below the given Major scale. Use whole notes, ascending only. (2 points)*

A♭ Major

_____ minor

13. *Write the key signature, then draw an ascending natural minor scale in the requested keys. (4 points)*

d minor

g♯ minor

MUSIC THEORY FOR SINGERS

14. *Label the following ornaments with their correct name.* (3 points)

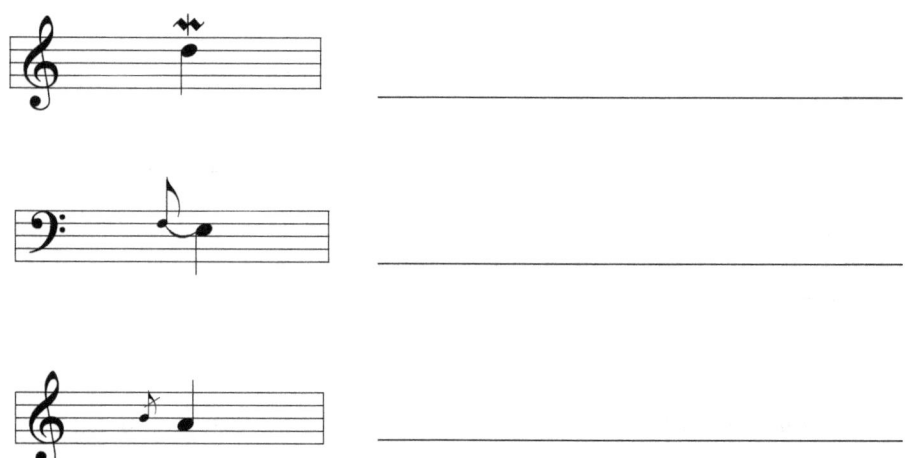

15. *Label the following chord progressions with the correct Roman numerals. Make sure to pay attention to the key signatures. In the Major example, chords are shown in inversions.* (8 points)

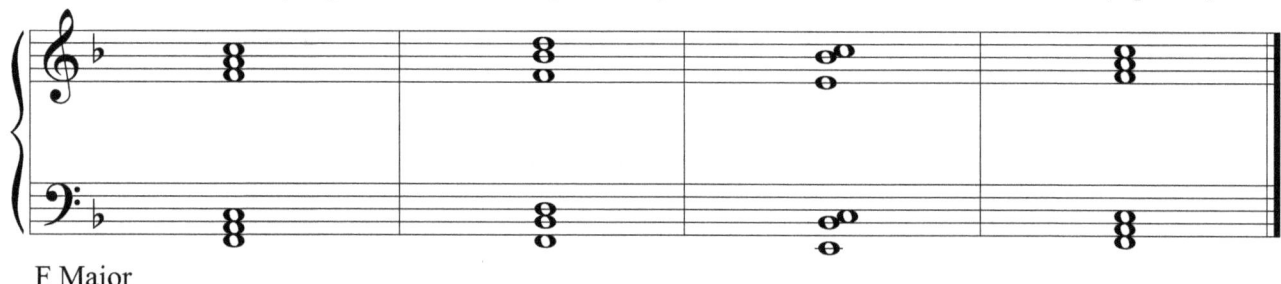

F Major

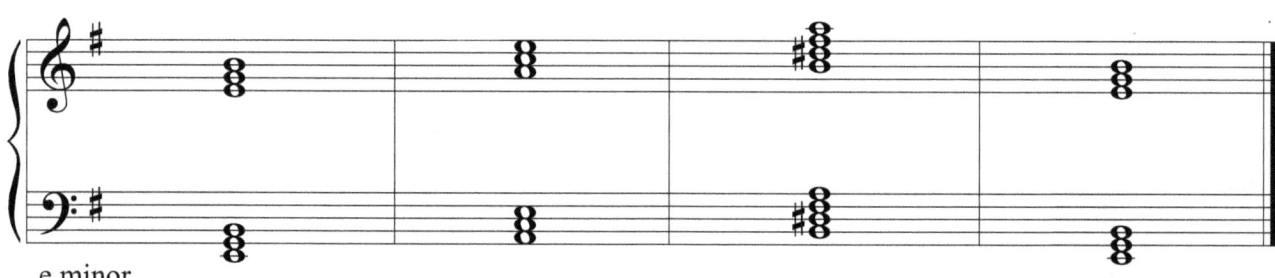

e minor

16. *Draw the correct chords according to the Roman numerals given. Make sure to use upper case Roman numerals for Major chords and lower case Roman numerals for minor chords. You may need to add an accidental on the dominant 7th chord in the minor key in order for the chords to be correct. You may use either root position or inversion chords. Pay attention to the key signatures. (8 points)*

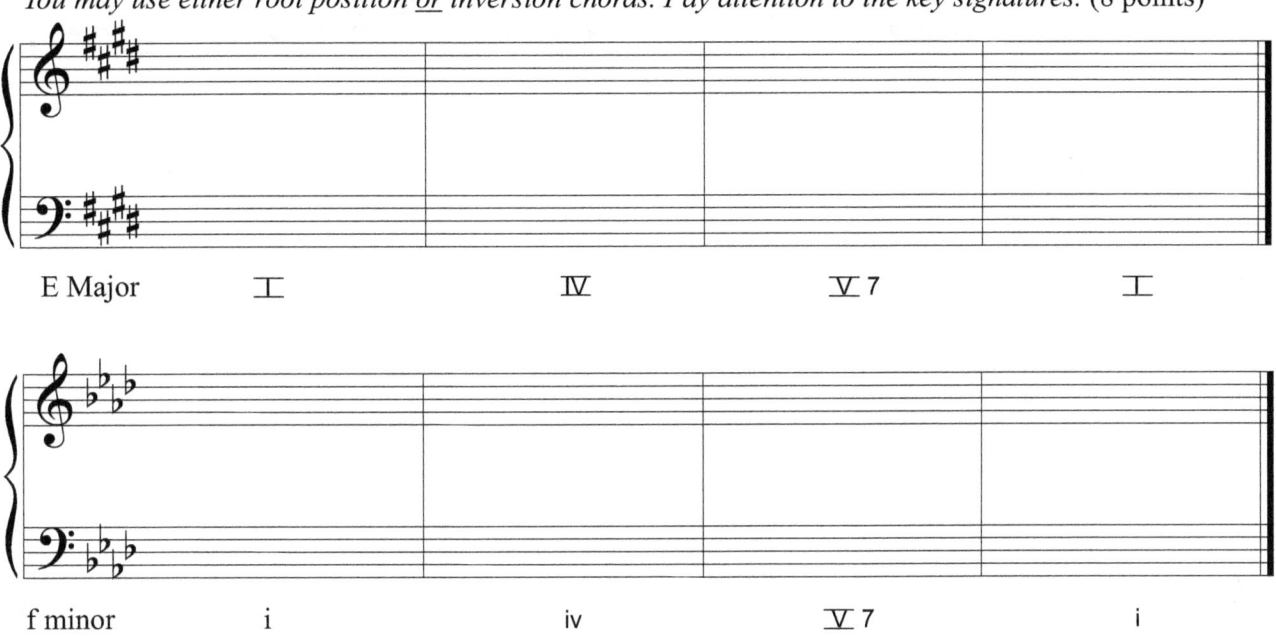

17. *Match the cadences with their correct name. All examples are in a Major key and in Root Position (3 points)*

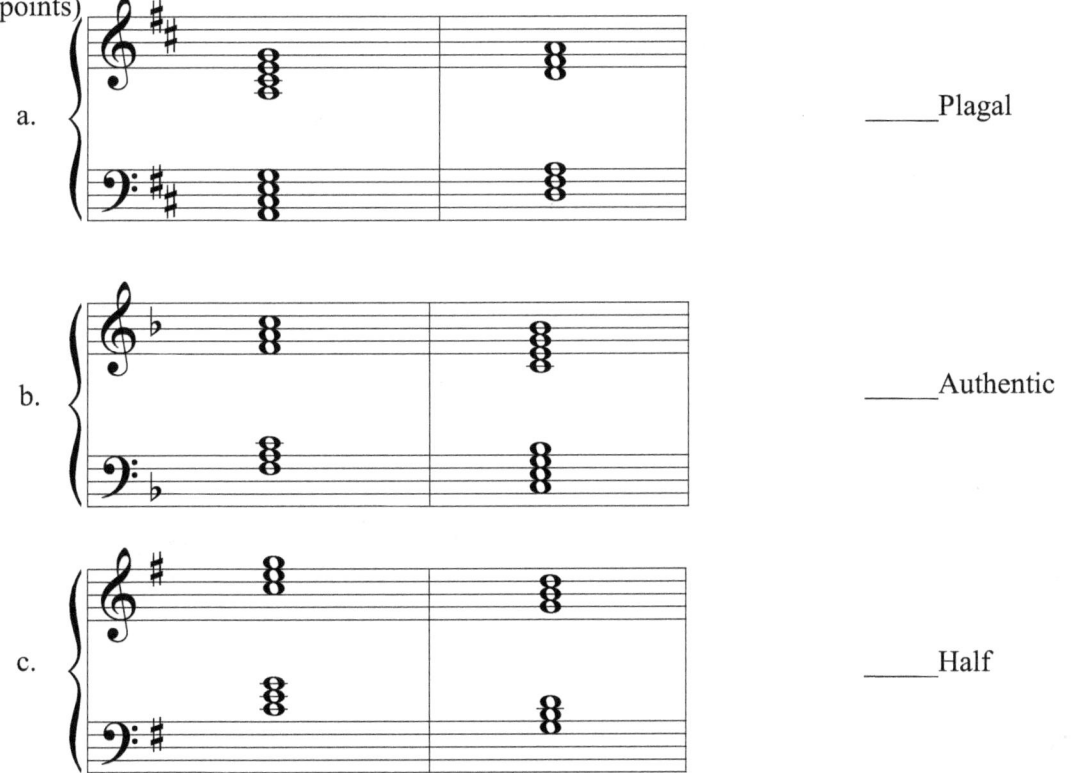

18. *Write the beats under the following rhythmic example.* (4 points)

19. *Write the note names and solfege under the notes in the following examples. Pay attention to the key signature. Add ♯/♭ if necessary.* (16 points)

Notes: _____

Solfege: _____

Notes: _____

Solfege: _____

Notes: _____

Solfege: _____

Notes: _____

Solfege: _____

20. *Match the voice classifications below with their definitions.* (11 points)

a. Coloratura Soprano   _____ (M) a voice that is richer and fuller and sometimes harsh, with a darker quality.

b. Lyric Soprano   _____ (F) the deepest female classical voice, falling between tenor and mezzo-soprano.

c. Dramatic Soprano   _____ (M) a male singing voice whose vocal range is equivalent to a contralto, mezzo soprano or soprano.

d. Mezzo Soprano   _____ (F) a coloratura soprano of great flexibility in high velocity passages, with great sustaining power.

e. Contralto (alto)   _____ (F) a very agile, light voice with a high range, capable of very fast coloratura; bel canto roles were written for this voice.

f. Countertenor   _____ (M) a light, agile tenor with ability to sing difficult passages of high velocity.

g. Lyric Tenor   _____ (M) a deep, heavy bass voice with an exceptionally low range, the lowest bass voice type.

h. Dramatic Tenor   _____ (M) a tenor with the brightness and height of a lyric tenor but a heavier vocal weight which can be "pushed" to dramatic climaxes.

i. Baritone   _____ (F) a type of operatic soprano voice who specializes in music with leaps, runs and trills.

j. Bass/Baritone   _____ (M) a type of male singing voice that lies between bass and tenor voices-the most common male voice.

k. Bass (Basso Profundo)   _____ (F) means "middle" soprano, with a darker color and ability to extend the range.

MUSIC THEORY FOR SINGERS

21. *Fill in the correct answer using the musical terms in this level.* (5 points)

a. An_____ is a song for solo voice within an opera or oratorio.

b. _____ means moving by half steps.

c. _____ means "light and fast" in French.

d. _____ is a smooth glide from one note to another.

e. A_____ is a solo passage, often technically difficult, usually near the end of a piece, either written by the composer or improvised by the performer.

22. *For the following questions, write "Granados, Fauré, or Copland" as your answer* (10 points)

a. This composer died when he was 49 years old._____

b. This composer's songs have been used as patriotic songs for the USA._____

c. This composer's teacher was the famous Nadia Boulanger._____

d. This composer was a member of the Société Nationale de Musique._____

e. This composer wrote music for films._____

f. This composer founded a music Academy in Barcelona, Spain._____

g. This composer was given a tribute concert in his honor._____

h. This composer wrote the opera *The Tender Land*._____

i. This composer performed at the White House for President Wilson._____

j. This composer taught at the Paris Conservatory of Music._____

Final Score:_____/100

REVIEW TEST: ANSWERS

1. What minor key is this song in?   __c__ minor

2. Define the term "Misterioso."   __mysterious__

3. What type of cadence is in the Bass clef in measures 3-4?   __Half__

4. What type of cadence is in the Bass clef in measures 7-8?   __Authentic__

5. How many times is this song sung?   ____ once

    __X__ twice

6. What type of ornament is in the vocal line in measure 1?   __Grace note__

7. Write the solfege syllables for the circled section in m.6.

    or   Do   Te   Le   Te   Sol
           La   Sol   Fa   Sol   Mi

8. *Write an ascending and descending chromatic scale beginning and ending on middle C. (2 points, one for ascending, one for descending)*

9. *Write the enharmonic note after the given note for each example. (4 points)*

10. *Add 3 bar lines and a double bar line to the following example. (4 points)*

11. *Add the missing time signature, then write the beats underneath the notes. (5 points-one for the time signature, one for each correct measure)*

1 & 2 & 3   1 e & a 2   3 &   1   2   3 e & a   1 & 2 & 3 &

12. *Name, then draw the relative minor scale in its natural form below the given Major scale. Use whole notes, ascending only. (2 points)*

f minor

13. *Write the key signature, then draw an ascending natural minor scale in the requested keys. (4 points)*

d minor

g# minor

MUSIC THEORY FOR SINGERS

14. *Label the following ornaments with their correct name.* (3 points)

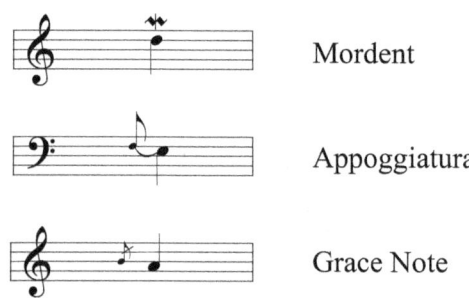

Mordent

Appoggiatura

Grace Note

15. *Label the following chord progressions with the correct Roman numerals. Make sure to pay attention to the key signatures. In the Major example, chords are shown in inversions.* (8 points)

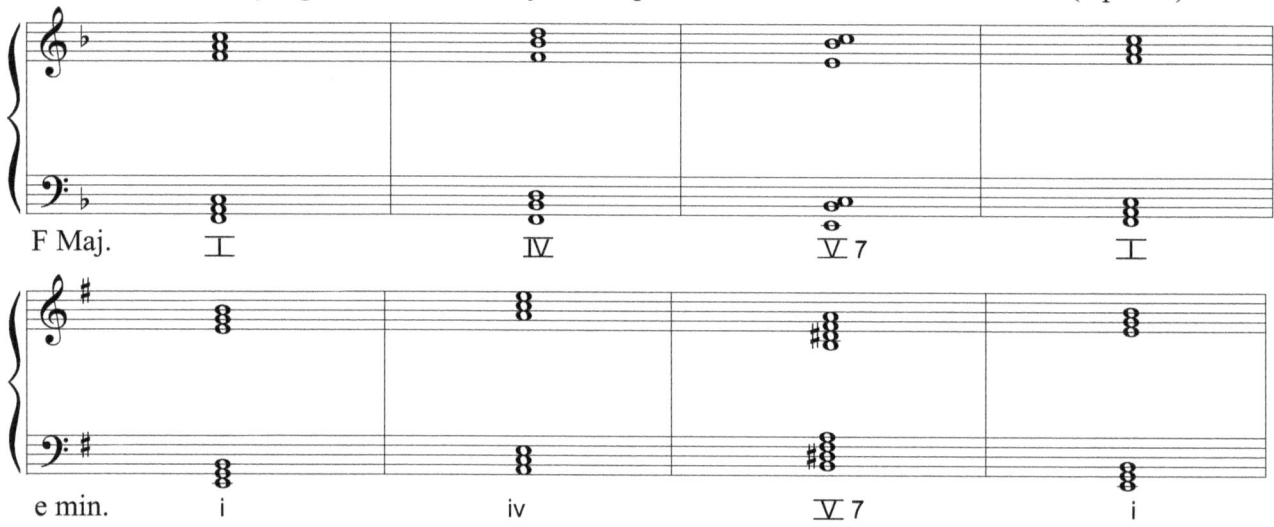

F Maj.   I   IV   V7   I

e min.   i   iv   V7   i

16. *Draw the correct chords according to the Roman numerals given. Make sure to use upper case Roman numerals for Major chords and lower case Roman numerals for minor chords. You may need to add an accidental on the dominant 7th chord in the minor key in order for the chords to be correct. You may use either root position or inversion chords. Pay attention to the key signatures.* (8 points)

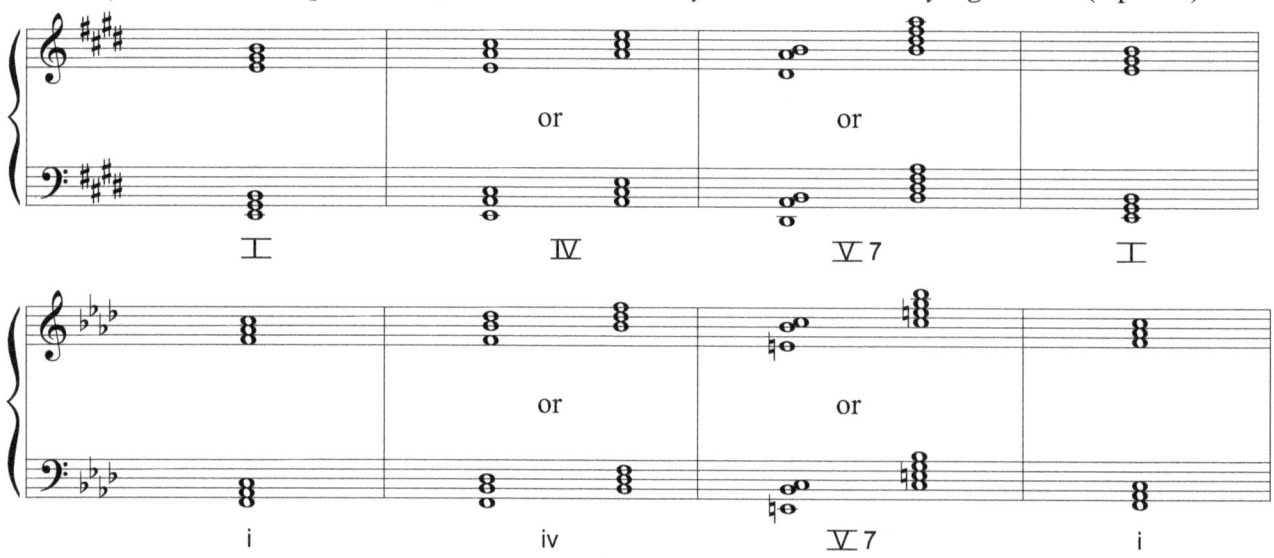

I   IV   V7   I

i   iv   V7   i

MUSIC THEORY FOR SINGERS

17. *Match the cadences with their correct name. All examples are in a Major key.* (3 points)

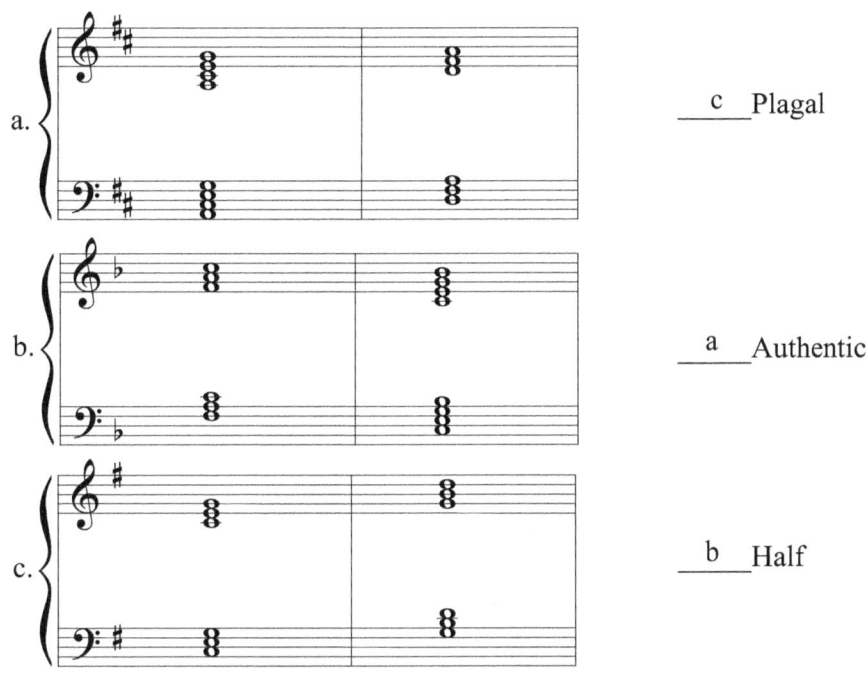

18. *Write the beats under the following rhythmic example.* (4 points)

19. *Write the note names and solfege under the notes in the following examples. Pay attention to the key signature.* (16 points)

20. *Match the voice classifications below with their definitions.* (11 points)

j
e
f
c
b
g
k
h
a
i
d

21. *Fill in the correct answer using the musical terms in this level.* (5 points)

a. An ____aria____ is a song for solo voice within an opera or oratorio.

b. ____chromatic____ means moving by half steps.

c. ____léger____ means "light and fast" in French.

d. ____portamento____ is a smooth glide from one note to another.

e. A ____cadenza____ is a solo passage, often technically difficult, usually near the end of a piece, either written by the composer or improvised by the performer.

22. *For the following questions, write "Granados, Fauré, or Copland" as your answer* (10 points)

a. This composer died when he was 49 years old. ____Granados____

b. This composer's songs have been used as patriotic songs for the USA. ____Copland____

c. This composer's teacher was the famous Nadia Boulanger. ____Copland____

d. This composer was a member of the Société Nationale de Musique. ____Fauré____

e. This composer wrote music for films. ____Copland____

f. This composer founded a music Academy in Barcelona, Spain. ____Granados____

g. This composer was given a tribute concert in his honor. ____Fauré____

h. This composer wrote the opera *The Tender Land*. ____Copland____

i. This composer performed at the White House for President Wilson. ____Granados____

j. This composer taught at the Paris Conservatory of Music. ____Fauré____

MUSIC THEORY FOR SINGERS

Level 1 Terms

accent -(>) – to emphasize or stress a note
bar line – a line that separates notes on the staff into measures
bass clef – also called F clef, it names the fourth line of the bass staff
chord - a group of 3 or more notes sounded at the same time
composer – a person who writes music
double bar line – two lines on a staff that indicate the end of a section or piece
fermata (🞑) – a hold or pause
key signature – sharps or flats written on the staff at the beginning of a piece to indicate the key
flat (♭) – lowers the pitch of a note one-half step
Folk Music - music that is learned by mouth, has no known composer, and was not initially written down
forte (*f*) – loud
interval - the distance between the pitches of two notes, sounded together or consecutively
legato – smooth and connected
measure – the space between two bar lines
piano (*p*) – soft
sharp (#) – an accidental that raises the pitch of a note one-half step
staccato – short and detached
staff – the five lines and four spaces on which music is written
time signature – the numbers at the beginning of a piece that indicate the number of beats in each measure and the type of note that receives one beat
treble clef – also called G clef, it names the second line of the treble staff

Level 2 Terms

a tempo – return to the original tempo
Baroque Period of Music - a term borrowed from architecture to describe Western European music written from 1600 to 1750
crescendo (⟨) – gradually getting louder
decrescendo (⟩) – gradually getting softer
dot (·) – added to a note, it increases the length of the note by 1/2 of its original value
fortissimo (*ff*) – very loud
ledger lines – short lines added above or below the staff so that notes can be written there
mezzo forte (*mf*) – medium loud
mezzo piano (*mp*) – medium soft
pianissimo (*pp*) – very soft
Renaissance Period of Music – in musical history, the period between 1425 and 1600
repeat signs – two dots placed before or after a double bar line, indicating a repeat of the music between the signs
ritardando (*rit.*) – becoming gradually slower
slur – a curved line connecting two or more different notes, indicating smoothness
tenuto (*ten.*) – sustain a note for its full value
tie – a curved line connecting two notes of the same pitch, which combines their values

Level 3 Terms
accidental – a flat, sharp, or natural sign
allegro – a lively, fast tempo
andante – a moderate, graceful, walking tempo
broken triad – three consecutive tones, Do-Mi-Sol
Classical period of music - a general term for the style of music written between 1750 and 1820
diminuendo (*dim.*) – gradually getting softer
dolce – sweetly
lento – slow
moderato – moderate tempo
molto – very
Musical Theatre/Broadway - a 20th Century form of theatre, combining music, songs, spoken dialogue and dance
natural (♮) – cancels the effect of a previous flat or sharp
poco a poco – little by little
sforzando (*sfz*) – a heavy, strong accent
simple meter – a time signature in which the basic beat can be divided by two

Level 4 Terms
adagio – a slow tempo falling between *largo* (slower) and *andante* (faster)
accelerando (*accel.*) – becoming faster
allegretto – a light, cheerful tempo, a bit slower than *allegro*
andantino – a little faster tempo than *andante*
con moto – with motion
diphthong – a vowel with two sounds
half step - the smallest musical interval between two adjacent notes in a 12-tone scale
Jazz music - began in America around 1900, influenced by African & European traditions. It incorporates blues, ragtime, swing, improvisation, syncopation & complex rhythms.
larghetto – a slow tempo, a little faster than *largo*
largo – slow and broad
meno mosso – less lively, slower
opera - a play in which the characters sing rather than speak, accompanied by instruments
più mosso – more lively, faster
rallentando (*rall.*) – becoming gradually slower
Romantic period of music - a 19th Century movement in the arts that influenced music from 1820 until 1920
sempre – always
senza – without
vocalise – a vocal exercise
whole step - the interval of a major 2nd; consists of 2 half steps

Level 5 Terms
alla breve / cut time (¢) – the same as 2 / 2 time
arietta – a short aria
bel canto – brilliant, lyric vocal style originating in Italy in the 18th & early 19th centuries
coda – a separate section at the end of a song, indicated by the symbol (⊕)
common time (C) – the same as 4 / 4 time
da capo (D.C.) – return to the beginning
da capo aria – a vocal form popular in the Baroque era, with an ABA form
D.C. al fine – return to the beginning and sing to the *fine*
dal segno (D.S.) – return to the sign (𝄋)
D.S. al fine – return to the sign and sing to the *fine*
D.S. al coda – return to the sign, proceed to the coda sign, then skip to the coda and finish the song
grazioso – gracefully
Late Romantic/Impressionistic period of music- a movement in European classical music, mainly in France, that began in the late 19th century and continued into the middle of the 20th century.
fine – end
operetta- a genre of light opera. The precursor to Musical Theatre
primary triad-one of three triads, (tonic, subdominant, dominant) built from thirds
repetition- a compositional technique accomplished by repeating the same melodic patterns exactly
sequence- a compositional technique consisting of repeating the same melodic patterns at a different pitch.
simile – to continue in the same manner
vivace – lively, quick, brisk tempo

Level 6 Terms
arpeggio – the notes of a chord sung or played in succession
art song – a vocal music composition, usually written for one voice with piano or orchestral accompaniment, typically set to poetry.
compound meter – a time signature in which the basic beat is divisible by three
Contemporary period of music-a general term for musical styles developed since 1900
espressivo – expressively, with emotion
fröhlich – (Ger.) glad, joyous
grace note- (♪) an unaccented ornamental note, which resolves quickly to the main note. Written in small type as an 8th note with a slash through it.
inversion- the result of shifting a note of an interval or chord so that the lowest note becomes the upper note
langsam – (Ger.) slowly
lebhaft – (Ger.) lively
lieblich – (Ger.) sweet, melodious
Lied – (Ger.) song
leise – (Ger.) soft
oratorio-a musical setting of a long, Biblically based text for soloists, chorus and orchestra
presto – very fast
ruhig – (Ger.) quiet
schnell – (Ger.) fast
strophic – a song in which the same music is repeated for all verses
through-composed – a song in which new music is composed for each verse of text
zart – (Ger.) delicately, softly

Level 7 Terms

animé – (Fr.)– moderately fast, animated

appoggiatura- ( ) an accented, non-harmonic note that resolves stepwise to a harmonic note, often written in small type

aria – a song for solo voice within an opera or oratorio

cadence- the series of notes or chords that ends a melody or section, giving the listener a sense of finality

cadenza – a solo passage, often technically difficult, usually near the end of a piece, either written by the composer or improvised by the performer

chanson – (Fr.) song

chromatic – moving by half steps

doucement – (Fr.) gently, softly

enharmonic – two notes that have the same pitch but different names

imitation-a compositional technique consisting of the overlapping repetition of a melody by two or more "voices"

léger – (Fr.) light and fast

lentement – (Fr.) slowly

libretto – the text, whether spoken or sung, of a dramatic vocal work

misterioso – mysteriously

modéré – (Fr.) moderately

mordent- ( ) an ornament where the main note and the note below are sung quickly in succession before returning to the main note.

portamento – a smooth glide from one note to another

recitative – a vocal number that mimics the inflections of speech, found primarily in operas and oratorios

rubato – freely speeding up or slowing down the tempo without changing the basic beat

triste – (Fr.) sad

vite – (Fr.) fast

Pronunciation Key for Diction

ə	banana, collide, put, oppose
'ə	humdrum, but
ə	immediately preceding \l\,\n\,\m\,\ŋ\, as in battle, mitten
ər	further, merger, bird
e	egg, chaotic
ɑ	father, tall
a	car, far
æ	mat, snap, cat, laugh
ā	day, fade, aorta
ä	cart, cot, father
aʊ	now, loud
ch	chin, nature \nā-chər\
ē	beat, nosebleed
ɛ	bet, red, peck
hw	when, whale
i	see
I	tip, banish
Ī	side, buy
ç	as in German *ich* and *Buch*
n	as in French *bon* \bō ⁿ
ŋ	sing, finger, ink
ō	bone, know, beau
ɔ	saw, all, caught
ʃ	short
ß	lass, pass
ɔ:ɪ	coin, destroy
th	thin, ether
<u>th</u>	then, either, this
ü	rule, youth
ʊ	pull, wood, book, fury \fyʊr-ē
ue	as in German *fünf*
uē	as in French *rue*
y	yard, mute \'myüt\
ʒ	casual, vision

Italian Diction for Singers:
As with any language, practicing speaking this language with an Italian accent will help with pronunciation.

Remember: No diphthongs! *Core* is pronounced Core-A, but without the E sound at the end of A. Another example is *Mio* is pronounced Mee-oh but without the oo sound and the end of O.

•I's are pronounced like E's. (ie) *Ma'mi* is pronounced Mamee

•All R's are rolled or flipped. If you cannot roll your R's, try something similar to a D. *Rosa* would sound similar to Dosa. Your tongue touches the top of your hard palate behind your top front teeth for the first letter.

•A "C" followed by an E or I is pronounced as a "CH." (ie) *Facil* is pronounced Facheel. Also *Dolce* is pronounced Dole-chay.
•A "CH" combo is pronounced as a K. (ie) *Chiaro* is pronounced Kee-ah-ro.

•When a word has a double consonant, you stop on the first consonant then continue. The best example of this is the word "*Pizza*." It's not pronounced PEEZA, it's pronounced PEETSA. Also *Quella* is Kwell-lah.

•A "G" at the beginning of a word is pronounced as an SH. (ie) *gentil* is pronounced shenteel.
•A "G" followed by an "L" is silent. (ie) *scegliera* is pronounced shay-lee-err-ah.
•A G followed by an H is pronounced as a Hard G…*Lunghezza* is pronounced Loon-get-tsa.
•A G followed by an I is pronounced as a J…*Giardi* is pronounced Jar-dee.

•*Que* is pronounced Kway.
•*Che* is pronounced Kay.

•An S followed by a C is pronounced as an SH. (ie) *s'angoscia* is pronounced zan-go-shee-ah.
•If an S is followed by a CH it's pronounced as SK. (ie) *scherzosa* is pronounced scare-tso-za.
•An S in between two vowels is pronounced as a Z. (ie) *ascosa* is pronounced ah-sko-za.

•An H at the beginning of a word is silent. (ie) *Hanno* is pronounced Ahn-no.

•A Z is pronounced like TS. (ie) *Danza* is pronounced Dawn-tsa.

• An "A" is pronounced as an "AH"

Spanish Diction for Singers

As with any language, practicing speaking this language with a Spanish accent will help with pronunciation.

Remember: No diphthongs! *Noche* is pronounced No-chay, but without the E sound at the end of A. Another example is *Mio* is pronounced Mee-oh but without the oo sound and the end of O.

- Roll all R's that begin a word.
- Flip all R's at the end of a word.
- Roll or flip all R's in the middle of a word depending on how it is usually pronounced.
- If the song was written by a Spanish composer, make all Y's, C's and T's soft. (ie)

hacer is pronounced Hather.

- Double LL's are pronounced as a Y. (ie) *Llega* is pronounced Yeah-gah.
- Pronounce every consonant with more emphasis than usual.
- Pay special attention to accents, and pronounce them as spoken.
- Pronounce J's with a small puff of air, in order for it to be audible, similar to an H. (ie)

Reja is pronounced Ray-ha.

- Always hold the first vowel when singing a word with a diphthong.
- *Que* is pronounced as Kay.
- *Che* is pronounced as Chay.
- An ñ is pronounced in the word Ke**nya**.
- A Y (the letter that stands for the word "and") is pronounced as an E.
- I's are pronounced as E's. *Mi* is pronounced as Mee.

German Diction for Singers:
As with any language, practicing speaking this language with a German accent will help with pronunciation.

*In German, vowel combinations will form sounds similar to diphthongs. "Blau" is pronounced Blah-oo. Much like the sound in the word "**Ouch**."*

- W's are pronounced as V's. (ie) *Werden* is pronounced Vair-den.
- V's are pronounced as F's. (ie) *Vater* is pronounced Faht-er.
- IE combinations are pronounced as an E. (ie) *Lied* is pronounced Leed.
- EI combinations are pronounced as an I. (ie) *Mein* is pronounced Mine.
- ü is called an Umlaud (the two dots). If you see this you form an "oo" with your lips, and say an "E."
- A Z at the beginning or end of a word is pronounced as a TS. (ie) *Zart* is pronounced Ts-art., *Herz* is pronounced Hair-ts
- A D at the end of a word is pronounced as a T. (ie) *Und* is pronounced Unt.
- A CH at the end of a word is pronounced with a lot of air, much like the sound of a hissing cat as in the word *ich*.
- Roll or flip all R's
- S's followed by a consonant is sounded as an SH. (ie) *stehn* is pronounced Shtain.
- E's are pronounced like an A as in Ate. (ie) *den* is pronounced Dane.
- J's are pronounced as a Y. (ie) *Jager* is pronounced Yay-ger.
- ß is a double S, "SS"

French Diction for Singers:

As with any language, practicing speaking this language with a French accent will help with pronunciation. All R's are forward and flipped when singing French. No back R's as when speaking French.

Remember: No diphthongs: "Les" is <u>Lay</u> without the e sound at the end.

**Much of French involves nasal sounds. You do not pronounce a lot of the ends of words. Instead you end them with a nasal sound. (ie) "Dans"= <u>Don</u> (without closing the N-touching the tip of your tongue to the roof of your mouth).

- Endings of words that are not pronounced are "s" "eil" "iens" "t" "ent" "ng"
- *Sommeil=<u>Somay</u>   Tes-<u>Tay</u>   Rayonnais=<u>Ray-oh-nay</u>*
- You do pronounce some endings of words if the following words starts with a vowel. *(vous avez)-* is pronounced <u>Vooz-Ah-vay</u>

- An E at the end of a word is a neutral sound much like "uh" (ie) *image*=<u>E-mah-guh</u> (g is pronounced like the S sound in the word <u>measure).</u> Other endings of words that have the neutral sound are: Es, eurs, re, ge, le, se

- If an X is at the end of a word and followed by a word that starts with a vowel, it's pronounced as a Z. (ie) *yeux etaient* = <u>Yooz-A-tay</u>

- The combination *heur* is like saying "earth" (with an open R and a dropped jaw) (ie) *l'heur* = <u>lehr (with a dropped jaw)</u>

- An accent over an e that is pointing up to the right is pronounced as an A. (ie) Hélas=<u>A-loss</u>

- U's have an E sound in them. (ie) *nues* = <u>new-uh</u>

- Some ends of words are pronounced as an A. (ie) "ais" and "aient"

- *Oi*=<u>W</u>   (as in *oui*-<u>we)</u>   *Toi*=<u>Twa</u>   *Voix*=<u>vwa</u>

- An I at the beginning of a word is nasal. *Incline*=<u>On-clean</u> (without closing the first n).

- An N proceeded by a vowel is nasal. (ie) *Long*=<u>Lon</u> (Nasal N without closing it).
    (ie) *Silence*=<u>See-lon-suh</u> (again without closing the N).

- An X at the end of a word is an Oh sound. (ie) *berceaux*=<u>bare-so</u>

- H's are silent (ie) *Hélas*=<u>A-loss.</u>

- *Qui*=<u>Key</u>

REFERENCES

Grout, Donald. *A History of Western Music.* New York, NY: W.W. Norton & Company, Inc., 1996.

Music Teachers' Association of California. *Certificate of Merit Voice Syllabus.* San Francsico: Music Teachers' Association of California, 2011.

Plantinga, Leon. *Romantic Music, A History of Musical Style in Nineteenth-Century Europe.* New York, NY: W.W. Norton & Company, Inc., 1984.

Piston, Walter. *Harmony, Fifth Edition.* New York, NY: W.W. Norton & Company, Inc., 1987.

Randel, Don Michael. *The Harvard Biographical Dictionary of Music.* Cambridge, Massachusetts: The Belknap Press of Harvard University Press, 1996.

Randel, Don Michael. *Harvard Concise Dictionary of Music.* Cambridge, Massachusetts: The Belknap Press of Harvard University Press, 1978.

Rushton, Julian. *Classical Music, A Concise History from Gluck to Beethoven.* London, England: Thames and Hudson Ltd., 1986.

The New Grove Dictionary of Music and Musicians.
http://www.oxfordmusiconline.com., 2011

www.ingramcontent.com/pod-product-compliance
Lightning Source LLC
Chambersburg PA
CBHW081136170426
43197CB00017B/2882